Raising a
Trailblazer

Rite-of-Passage Trail Markers
for Your Set-Apart Teens

Raising a Trailblazer is filled with wisdom, creativity, humor, and spiritual substance. You will be inspired to help your teens become the people God created them to be. There is so much insight in how to be an effective parent that· it should be required reading for all parents. It is a delightful book!

Rebecca Pippert Molenhouse
Mother of two, author, speaker, founder and director of Salt Shaker Ministries

. . . .

Virginia is herself a trailblazer: innovator, pioneer, originator, ground breaker, forerunner. A person who challenges status-quo and has always intentionally blazed a path for herself and her family in keeping with their faith and predetermined values. Through Home Improvement Ministries, she and Paul have helped countless families do the same. If you want to raise a set-apart teen, an independent thinker in the midst of a culture urging them to blend in so they fit in, you will find Virginia's suggestions invaluable. Implementing these trail markers with your teens will leave them with a stronger sense of personal value and purpose as they navigate their unique path in life.

Deb McCormick
Mother of three boys, founder and director of TeamedUp

. . . .

Once in a while you come across a book that you would like to keep as an ongoing reference tool for raising children. This is most certainly one of those treasures. Virginia and her three transparent daughters share invaluable principles and ideas for raising a truly set-apart teen and hope for nurturing a young adult into the arms of Jesus. The importance of purity, affirmation, grace and truth, and helping your child discover God's purposes for his or her life are a far cry from anything this world will offer. If you are looking for a counter-cultural approach to these precious years in your child's life, then it's not an accident that you're holding this book.

Emily Williams
Mother of four, bride of Grant Williams, 10 year NFL veteran

. . . .

With clarity and conviction, Virginia provides guidance for parents desiring to raise a child with godly purpose and direction. With the eyes of a prophet, the heart of a mom, the insight of a counselor, and the understanding of a friend, parents find hope and a plan that works. I recommend parents of young children begin now to read this book so they can prepare for and confidently navigate the oft-times confusing years of adolescence. Virginia doesn't just tell us how, but she models for us how parents can find their teenager not only desiring a deep relationship with them, but also coveting their insight above the clamor of the world and their peers.

Jan Northington
Mother of four, author, speaker

I am grateful for Virginia's heart and vision for mentoring our children through the exciting yet very challenging teen years. It was Virginia's vision-casting that inspired my husband and me to conduct blessing ceremonies for both our son and daughter. These tangible rite-of-passage ceremonies allowed us to speak truth into the lives of our children and affirm the values of purity, holiness, humility, and grace.

Barbara X. Becker
Home-schooling mother of two, Creative Memories representative

. . . .

From the first page of *Raising a Trailblazer*, Dr. Virginia Friesen wisely mentors us as we guide our children up the trails of life, pause to celebrate their progress at critical ages, and aim for the "summit" of maturity in Christ. This groundbreaking book begs to be read, reread, and shared with all parents who yearn for more than the status quo.

Linda Brown, MD
Home-schooling mother of four, part-time medical doctor

. . . .

Dr. Virginia Friesen has offered inspiring and practical tools for parents who want to usher their kids into the kind of adulthood they dream for them . . . one built on the foundations of grace, truth, and purpose, and saturated with love. After reading this book, I am almost looking forward to the teenage years with my three sons.

Jan Christian Martinet
Mother of three, one of the mentors in the Friesen girls' lives

. . . .

Virginia Friesen offers in this book tremendous insight and practical wisdom into the windows of opportunity—rite-of-passage trail markers—in our children's lives. Her concepts are creative and transferable and will help us guide our children into the hope and future God has planned for them.

Anne Gaddini
Mother of four, wife of Gary, lead pastor of Peninsula Covenant Church

. . . .

In this treasure-filled book, Virginia Friesen not only offers practical ways to commemorate birthdays with love and attention for those critical coming-of-age teen years, she presses into each observance precious teaching toward the future filled with truth, hope, and vision. Her wonderful "trail markers" for the journey are far more than mere blazes to show the way; she has leveraged them to become both vistas and feeding stations.

Barbara Steele
Mother of three, founding board member of Mom to Mom Ministries

Raising a Trailblazer

Rite-of-Passage Trail Markers for Your Set-Apart Teens

by

Dr. Virginia Friesen

Home Improvement Ministries
Bedford, Massachusetts

Raising a Trailblazer
Rite-of-Passage Trail Markers for Your Set-Apart Teens
Virginia Friesen

Copyright © 2008 by Dr. Virginia Friesen
Cover & Interior design by David Eakin, Troop Media, LLC
Copy editing by Jim Craft
Final editing by Guy and Barbara Steele

Cover photos by Virginia Friesen, taken while hiking the Schilthorn in Lauterbrunnen, Switzerland, on daughter Julie's 21st birthday "life purpose" rite of passage. Family photo taken on top of Half Dome, September 2, 2003.

ISBN-13: 978-0-9789931-3-9
ISBN-10: 0-9789931-3-6

Home Improvement Ministries
209 Burlington Road, Suite 105
Bedford, MA 01730

Visit us on the web at: www.HIMweb.org

Printed in the United States of America   3/08TPS4000

Dedication

To my three intrepid, persevering,
and responsive "hikers"—
Kari, Lisa, and Julie.
I love you the whole wide world . . .
and then some.

Table of Contents

Foreword

All of us look forward to milestones in our lives when we can look back and give thanks for what we have learned, set our sights on where we need to be stretched, and have others affirm where they see growth in us. In this book, my friend Virginia Friesen shares tried-and-tested ideas for making an adolescent child feel challenged, valued, loved, and affirmed at four different junctures during the teen years.

I've had the opportunity to observe the difference this has made in all three of Paul and Virginia's daughters, Kari, Lisa, and Julie. They have become women who are bright lights in the kingdom of Christ, a joy to their parents and friends, and a gift to their communities. And each shares a deep bond with her mother. I've looked forward to the day when Virginia would put her experiences in print so that other mothers can do the same.

The *gift* that Virginia has eagerly given her teens includes these four passages: at age **thirteen**, the "Value of Purity"; at **sixteen**, the "Value of Affirmation"; at **eighteen**, the "Value of Truth and Grace"; climaxing at age **twenty-one** with the "Value of Purpose." How each passage is celebrated is tailor-made to fit each child's temperament, spirituality, and emotional level. And while each passage is challenging, it's also full of fun! These four different seasons note the progress of each child's maturing in character and faith, and these can then be celebrated through unique activities, words, experiences, and affirmations—all designed to proactively say "well done."

I wish I had had these ideas when we were raising our children. Read with anticipation that this might make being a parent of teenagers inspiring, fun, and transforming.

—*Gail MacDonald*
Peace Ledge
Canterbury, New Hampshire

And from the Three Hikers

Julie:

My mom is one of the most authentic, empathetic, intentional women I have ever met. She has modeled what it means to fear the Lord and to respond to His call. She has prioritized mothering, which is so evident in the way she has lived. I can only hope that one day I can be half the mom my mom has been. She writes this book out of experience and love. As one who has experienced the rites of passage mentioned in these pages, I am forever grateful.

It is so easy to live life in the moment, reactively rather than proactively. In *Raising a Trailblazer*, the reader is challenged to live intentionally in order to gain the most from important milestones in life. These rites of passage have transformed my life by causing me to pause at significant junctures and evaluate life both reflectively and prospectively. They have also taught me to smell the roses along the trail, which is an important lesson to learn in our very fast-paced, results-driven culture. I will treasure these trail marker moments all my life.

—*Julie Friesen*
San Luis Obispo, California

Lisa:

Growing pains are one of life's guarantees. Our culture recognizes that the teen to early adult years are challenging and often tumultuous; however, not much has been done to help teens make these formative years more purposeful. In her book *Raising a Trailblazer*, my mom not only recognizes this challenge but offers a concrete solution. She proposes taking bold, countercultural steps not just to survive these years but to make them count positively.

I am blessed to have been one of the "guinea pigs" for this book. These values-driven trail markers have helped shape who I am today and who I am becoming. This is not a book of lofty, unattainable ideals, but of practical suggestions for ordinary people on life's journey. My mom is a woman of immense character who lives what she teaches. What she has written in this book reflects the manner in which she lives her life. I am incredibly blessed to have her as my mother as well as my best friend. May these words encourage you as you and your teen journey together.

—*Lisa Friesen*
San Luis Obispo, California

Kari:

I am the oldest of the three Friesen girls and therefore am privileged to be the *first* to have experienced the rite-of-passage trail markers in our family. I don't remember the type of cake or what gifts I got at many of my birthdays, but if you ask me about turning ages thirteen, sixteen, eighteen, and twenty-one, I can tell you every detail. Each celebration was filled with meaningful gifts and unforgettable memories that have shaped who I am today.

I now work full time with youth, and it breaks my heart to see how influenced teens are by today's culture. *Raising a Trailblazer* gives practical tools for parents to become the primary developers in their children's lives. Today's youth need a solid understanding of the importance of purity, affirmation, grace, truth, and purpose—all character concepts that will shape them for life.

Personally, these trail markers came at significant times in my life when I was questioning who I really was and what I wanted my life to be marked by. I look back at each trail marker and see God's hand of direction and grace on my life. He used those celebrations to guide me toward the goal of becoming more like Him. To this day, my trail marker gifts are my most treasured possessions. For example, I still go back and read letters from the affirmation book I received for my sixteenth birthday.

I encourage you to read, learn, and then act. It's never too late to come alongside your children and help shape them into who God calls them to be.

In closing, I have to brag about the author—my mom, my mentor, and my ex-best-friend (my husband now holds the "best friend" position). The words in this book are a reflection of my mom's heart. She (along with my dad) raised the three of us girls to be women who understand who we are in Christ and the lives we are called to live. The words are written from true-life experience, as my parents battled against cultural influences to raise us to be women of God. I would not be where I am today without her constant love and devotion to the development of my character and my heart for the Lord. I am so blessed to be one of Virginia's girls, and I pray that I will one day be as loving and as intentional with my children as she has been with us. She is truly a woman who reflects the heart of God in how she loves and cares for God's people.

I pray that you will be able to see her heart on these pages. This book is a treasure to read, to understand, and to live by. God bless your reading!

—*Kari Friesen Garcia*
Sacramento, California

And, finally, from Paul

On December 15, 1975, when I asked Virginia Collins to spend the rest of her life with me, I knew I was marrying a beautiful, godly, fun woman. I had already observed that. I also expected she would be a wonderful mother to our children; I just didn't know how exceptionally wonderful. At ages 27, 25, and 22, our three girls love the Lord, each other, and us. I don't know of anything more a parent could wish for. Virginia's intentionality in parenting our girls has more to do with where they are today than anything else in their lives, humanly speaking. I have tried to be a good dad, but Virginia has been a fantastic mom. She has made them a huge focus of her life. She has modeled for them what a woman of God looks like and done it in such a way they have each fallen in love with Jesus and are now following Him fully.

The book you hold in your hands is not a "four easy steps to raising children" book. There is nothing easy about it, nor is it automatic. What this book does give you, however, is a glimpse into a mom's heart for her children and her decisions to help her children look forward to growing up responsibly and well. The book is largely about relationships. You may decide to have your child go on a parent-child weekend at 13, have a video collage at 16, receive an engraved bible at 18, and go on a road trip with you at 21. The details of what you do are not critical. But the values you are striving to instill and celebrate are *essential* to equipping them for life.

Our verse as a couple comes from 3 John 4, "I have no greater joy than to hear that my children are walking in the truth." I have a great deal of joy as I watch our children walk through life. I believe this book can contribute to your experiencing such joy yourself. Happy hiking, and don't forget to keep your eyes on the Trail Master, from whose heart comes the values inscribed on each trail marker. The One who leads you can be trusted. He wants you and your children to experience all the unbelievably beautiful and meaningful places along the trail. To Him be the glory.

Acknowledgments

As is true with any hike, there is a beginning. My deepest gratitude and respect, therefore, are given to my parents, RADM and Mrs. Frank C. Collins, Jr., USN-ret., who made the very gutsy and difficult decision to reject the doctor's advice to terminate my mother's fourth pregnancy in five years due to her chronic kidney problems. Though far from family and friends as they served in the U.S. Navy in Panama, they chose to trust God for the outcome and continue the pregnancy. That pregnancy produced me. I will always be aware of the grace and trust that has cocooned my life since its inception.

The writing of this book has been supported by many dear friends and mentors. Gail MacDonald, one of my most faithful mentors, first convinced me to write this. She has encouraged me through the process, and I am so grateful. Cynthia Heald, my long-time mentor-by-book, was kind enough to read and endorse this book.

Deb McCormick, inspiring friend and founder of TeamedUp, and Helen Challener, faithful kindred spirit friend of over thirty years, both spent countless hours poring over the manuscript and guiding the evolution of the book. I will forever be grateful for their sacrifice of time and the gift of their talents.

Jan Northington, Gordon and Barbara Becker, Amy Kardel, Linda Brown, Emily Williams, Kimary Pomphrett, Robin Kraning, Becky Molenhouse, Melanie Bilazarian, Anne Gaddini, Jan Christian Martinet, Nirma Raffi, Dawn Amico, Christina Swanson, Doug Macrae, and Phil and Linda Sommerville have all been readers of the manuscript and have given me invaluable input. I am so blessed by each one's contribution.

Jim Craft was a delightful and insightful editor, and David Eakin lent his creativity to the design and layout. Guy and Barbara Steele did the final editing, and it's hard to imagine anyone better than them for finishing touches.

And finally, to the little band of hikers with whom I am privileged to be journeying through life, Kari, Lisa, and Julie, and to my hiking partner since 1976, Paul. I just don't have the words (shocking, I know!) to express the depth of my appreciation and love for each of you. The trail has been varied, surely, through the years: easy and fully enjoyable at times, and challenging and difficult at others. We've experienced the beauty of vistas that look like the glory of God in all its fullness, and we've had moments where we could see nothing through the dark and shadowy times of loss, confusion, and hurt. There is no one in the world I would've rather traveled with than the four of you.

Chapter 1
The Trailhead

Trust in the Lord with all your heart
and lean not on your own understanding;
in all your ways acknowledge Him
and He will make your paths straight.
Proverbs 3:5-6

"How do I get from here to there?" is a question that surfaces time and time again during the journey of life. Whether it be finances (from instability to security), maturity (from childishness to wisdom), or contentment (from grumbling to gratitude), we are challenged along the way to stay on the right paths that lead to life-giving places.

Nowhere are these transitions more difficult and more important than in the raising of our kids. Getting children from early adolescence to adulthood successfully, while maintaining personal sanity and staying connected with them, is thought by many parents to be impossible. There is ample evidence that the teen trail is fraught with dangers which threaten the emotional, spiritual, and physical well-being of our children. Teenage rebellion, combined with the (perceived or real) generation gap, and poor choices with long-term effects, describe the journey of far too many teenagers.

In *Raising a Trailblazer*, I propose a series of rite-of-passage celebrations—"Trail Markers" at the significant birthdays of thirteen, sixteen, eighteen, and twenty-one—to help guide our maturing children "from here to there" in positive, life-giving ways. With a desire to encourage our own three children at these important birthdays and to reinforce that it was good to be journeying together toward the summit of their childhood, my husband and I developed these rite-of-passage celebrations. Our hope was that these trail markers would contribute to preparing our girls for "the rest of their lives" which would, by God's grace, be lived according to His unique design. Our prayer was that by the time they reached the "summit," they would be firmly established in their biblical convictions, their global compassion, and their confidence and completeness in Christ. We desired that they would know that God's personal love for them was transforming them into people who would make a positive difference in this world as well as in eternity. Each of the trail markers would emphasize and reinforce a value necessary for the journey. We were committed to *preparing our children for the trail, rather than the trail for our children.*

If you're like us, parenting may well be the hardest thing you have ever done. Honestly, that caught us by surprise. How clearly my husband Paul and I remember our own naive expectations as we awaited the birth of our first child. We had read the books. We had both been raised in good Christian homes. Both sets of our parents had thriving marriages. We were prepared.

Unfortunately, our child had *not* read the books. She did not know that she was supposed to sleep much more than be awake as a newborn. She did not know that if she were fed, clean, and dry, she should be perfectly content. Those early days gave us the first indications that parenting was not going to be as easy as the books made it seem.

And so began our parenting journey. As exasperating as it was at times, there were many more good moments than bad moments and many more joys than sorrows. At times we had fleeting thoughts of *Why did we intentionally bring children into this world?* Thankfully, we found that these short-lived doubts were well outweighed by the wonderful, sanctifying benefits of raising children.

And then they became teens. In general, the press about the teen years is discouraging at best. We are almost set up by our culture to expect our teens to be characterized by out-of-control, rebellious, and disrespectful behavior. "Helpful advice" that contributed to our fear and insecurity regarding teen parenting included such wisdom as Mark Twain's suggestion: "When a kid turns 13, stick him in a barrel, nail the lid shut, and feed him through the knot hole. When he turns 16, plug the hole." While such advice is good for a laugh, it reminds us that the teen years are often tough for children and for parents, and that there are sometimes more questions than answers.

How can we best seize these years so they will be characterized as the "age of opportunity" for our families? Can we succeed at positively guiding our children through their adolescent years? Is it truly possible to actually *enjoy* the teen years and this part of the trail on the journey? Or should we all invest in barrel-making industries?

By the grace of God, my husband Paul and I found that we could seize the opportunities of those years, exploit them positively, and guide our teens with loving and wise biblically driven values.

Some of you may be thinking, *That's easy for you to say! I don't have a Christian heritage. The legacy I received from my parent(s) is not one I wish to pass on. I feel thoroughly inadequate. I'm barely making it day-to-day, much less thinking of what's down the trail.*

Take a deep breath! You do not need to have a Christian heritage in order to pursue the principles of trailblazing. You did not choose your family of origin any more than we did. And though our Christian heritage is a generational legacy, these trail markers were new for our children. Both sets of our parents had more than enough on their plates just to keep their many children clothed, fed, and remembered on their birthdays!

Each of you can, however, choose to give your children a Christian heritage and launch into the next generation with a God-honoring legacy. By God's grace, you can raise trailblazers who will hike a less-traveled trail that will be a testament to the power and reality of God and His plans.

A *trailblazer.* What's that? Simply put, it is someone who forges a new trail. One who takes the trail less traveled. One who takes the challenge of not just "going with the flow" and ending up in the catch basin with everyone and everything else, but seeks a route that brings one to a place where the call on and purpose of one's life can be fulfilled. A trailblazer is a pioneer— someone who does not settle for the status quo or embrace the *modus operandi* of our culture.

The pull of culture is great. The relentless assault of secular humanism, materialism, and narcissism has a persistent, desensitizing effect on even the most ardent followers of Christ. Over time, perhaps imperceptibly at first, we settle for values that may be slightly better than the culture at large but increasingly distant from biblical values. A trailblazer is intentionally out of step with culture in order to be in step with God's call.

How does a parent raise a trailblazer? Ideally, the process starts when a child is young. Parents must train their children to have strong character and strong convictions. The life lessons impressed on their children's young hearts and minds will be foundational in equipping them for the trail they will blaze during their adolescent years.

If your children are no longer in the single-digit ages, do not despair! It is not too late! You are still in a position to model for your adolescents that *you* are growing, learning, and changing. This speaks volumes to a child who thinks (or at least thinks that *you* think) that parents know everything, are set in their ways, and will never change.

Whether you have little ones or almost grown ones, the question still remains: How do we guide and inspire our hikers to *want* to blaze such a trail? Because few of us who are in the parenting stage of our lives feel that we had great trail guides in our own families of origin, it might be overwhelming or depressing to imagine how to do it differently.

First, let me say how these hopes will *not* be fulfilled. Raising trailblazers will not be the result of perfect parenting (or even of reading this book!). There are no perfect parents. Raising trailblazers will not happen because you have a formula that guarantees results. There are neither formulas nor guarantees that work any more effectively than overnight weight-loss programs. Raising trailblazers will not happen because you manage to cloister your hikers and protect them from all evil on the trail. Remember that the evil is within, in the form of our fallen human nature, as well as outside. And raising a trailblazer definitely will not happen if you believe that as long as it *looks* like everything is good, it is. This approach is akin to putting on cheap tennis shoes to hike a long distance: they wear thin quickly.

Our hopes to raise our children to become godly, Christian trailblazers will be fulfilled only when we place them in the hands of the One who has the ultimate power to transform. With our hope firmly rooted in Him and His Word, we can positively and optimistically embrace the role of guide for our trailblazers. How? By pursuing Him personally and actively. By reading and studying His Word. By inviting godly mentors to help guide our journey. By prayerfully seeking wisdom. By humbly admitting our failures, repenting of them, and changing. By exchanging appearance management for authenticity.

Still, there are no guarantees. Unfortunately, not all children arrive at the summit you are steering them toward. Some experience injuries along the way that hinder their progress. Some will ignore the signs and pursue paths that will take them far from the trail markers you have prayed and prepared them for. Perhaps your child is not pursuing godliness, despite your hopes and prayers. Is there any point in doing these rite-of-passage trail markers for a wayward child? Our answer is a resounding "Yes!" With sensitivity to your teen, adapt the ideas in this book to remind him or her how much he or she is loved—and of how good it is to hike together.

Our role as parents is to live out our faith consistently and authentically day by day in our homes and to provide an environment most conducive to our children's responding positively to Jesus. *We cannot make our children say yes to Him.* In the end, they must choose for themselves. God has given His people the freedom to choose between good and evil, between Him and the ways of the world. That means that our children have the freedom to choose, and we most likely will not like all the choices they make! In fact, if our children were to make all the decisions we wanted them to, they would be puppets—not prophets. Puppets always need to be attached to puppeteers. Prophets are attached to God, functioning beautifully without us.

By God's grace, they will choose Him. For today, however, the most important thing you can do is to keep seeking Him yourself. This will equip you to blaze a trail with your teens that will distinguish them from the masses of confused, undirected, purposeless, and oftentimes rebellious peers. The trail, identified by trail markers, will by God's grace lead all of us ultimately to our true home: the heart of God.

Chapter 2
Prepare to Hike

Commit to the Lord whatever you do,
and your plans will succeed.
Proverbs 16:3

We set out at 1:30 in the morning, full of energy, excitement, expectation, and, admittedly, a little fear. The destination? The top of Half Dome, one of the magnificent geological formations in California's Yosemite National Park, which stands 8,836 feet above sea level and is 9.2 miles from the trailhead. The Friesen Five (ranging in age from 19 to 54) had hiked Half Dome for the first time the previous year—and in broad daylight. A night hike promised adventure, few people on the popular trail, and cooler temperatures.

Starting at the trailhead, we were faced with a decision: Should we hike the tried-and-true John Muir Trail or the slightly shorter Mist Trail? Confident that both trails would be well marked with trail markers and having hiked the John Muir Trail the year before, we decided to try the latter. After all, we reasoned, the trail markers would be our guide.

Trail markers serve at least two important functions for hikers. Primarily, they keep the hiker going in the right direction and on the right path. Additionally, they mark the distance along the way; each trail marker reminds hikers how far they've hiked and how far they have to go. A hiker can feel elation or discouragement at any given marker, but at least he or she knows the score: Three miles down, six to go. Six miles down, three to go. The markers provide important information to all who pass by and take notice. They remind hikers that they are getting closer to the destination. Trail markers also alert hikers if they have strayed from the intended trail.

Armed with flashlights, water, and snacks, we started hiking the trailhead common to both the John Muir Trail and the Mist Trail. It wasn't long before we discovered how oddly different the trail seemed in the dark than it had in the light. Starlight provided the only illumination on this seemingly moonless night, as the waning moon didn't contribute any measure of brightness until 4:00 a.m.

Our goal was to be atop Half Dome before the sun wakened the world, so we could witness the majesty of sunrise from a most spectacular viewpoint. Standing between us and that summit was 9.2 miles of what we thought would be a fairly well-marked trail. Being lifelong outdoors enthusiasts and in at least semi-good shape, we had few concerns about making it to the top. Hiking together has been a way of life for us. Far beyond purposes of getting a good workout in the beauty of God's creation, we had discovered significant life lessons through the years during our hiking journeys. All five of us have added to our "mind journals" (memories) insightful entries discovered while hiking. For our family, hiking is a clear metaphor for life.

Lisa Writes

Hiking has always been a family affair. From our never-to-be-forgotten young childhood "survival hike" on Catalina Island to our Half Dome ascent, and hundreds of miles in between, we have been committed to staying together on the trail as a family. As we have hiked in the community of family, we have learned to encourage one another in spite of and in the midst of our circumstances (exhaustion, hunger, thirst, and pain). In the process of the journeys, we have learned so much about ourselves and each other. We have experienced that hiking together requires sacrifice and sensitivity. When we were little, our parents waited for and encouraged us. Now that we are young adults, we wait for and encourage them! One of the best parts of hiking is that it has allowed us to get away from the busyness of life and to gain or regain perspective. It has built strength into the fabric of our family.

On that dark September night, we learned how important trail markers are to the hiker. And we learned it the hard way. With soaring spirits and echoes of laughter, the first portion of the hike was a breeze, and the first trail marker came quickly. 1.3 miles down, 7.9 to go! We thoroughly enjoyed facing this challenge together, and in such an unorthodox fashion; we hardly noticed that the Mist Trail was becoming less distinct. Because it crossed close to the flow of the falls (thus earning its name "Mist Trail"), we discovered that the granite steps and path often blended in with the surroundings. In the darkness, it was difficult to know *if* we were actually still on the trail. At one junction, the trail seemed to turn right . . . or was it to the left? We made our best guess, headed to the left, and hoped it was the correct choice. Doubts increased as the "trail" became less and less discernible. Silently, I thought, *Soon we'll come upon a trail marker which will confirm our direction . . . or not.* Our laughter and bantering submerged beneath our unspoken but rising fears, and our desperate search for a trail marker was unsuccessful. Without a trail marker, we felt lost.

We wandered in the darkness for awhile, finally admitting our fear. We were lost indeed. Ever the optimist, my husband, Paul, assured us that we would be fine, but I detected some concern in his usually confident voice. In the dark of the night, shadows cast by trees and other rock formations seemed sinister, and creaks and groans were amplified frightfully in the stillness of the natural amphitheater. It was downright eerie. Time passed slowly and minutes felt much longer. We were all still straining to find the trail—or even better, a trail marker—when, finally, we succeeded in carefully retracing our steps to the juncture of our last turn and headed in the opposite direction.

Thankfully, it was not many minutes on our redirected journey before the trail became more clearly defined. We joyously let loose with ecstatic whoops and hollers which echoed off the granite walls of the mountain when we came upon the trail marker, confirming our location and announcing that we were halfway to the top. For the rest of the hike, we managed to stay on the flashlight-lit path, grateful for the signs which marked the way. The trail markers, each in succession, consoled us in affirming that we were going in the right direction, that we were making great progress, and that we were definitely closer to reaching our goal.

Had we gotten lost on Half Dome, and been forced to survive by fending off bears, sharing just tablespoons of water, and eating pine cones for sustenance, this family adventure would possibly have wound up as a *Reader's Digest* "Drama in Real Life" story. Instead our family drama (rather than melodrama!) remains a fitting metaphor for the rite-of-passage trail markers we have developed for our daughters.

Julie Writes

I remember starting off that morning so excited, without a thought of fear on the radar, because I trusted Dad so much to lead us. When we lost the trail and Dad went on ahead, I remember the first wave of fear as I realized we could be stuck in the middle of the forest all night and Dad would not be with us. I was so relieved when he rejoined us, and we worked our way back to our last turn point *together*. Four and a half hours after we started our memorable night hike, we sat on top of Half Dome watching the majesty and wonder of the rising sun. And four hours after that, we were back down in Yosemite Valley having successfully achieved our goal. It was one of the most exhilarating feelings to finish the hike together, as a team.

Kari Writes

Looking back, it occurs to me how easily fear can paralyze a person to the point where he or she cannot experience some of the most majestic things in life. That Half Dome night hike would have never happened had my parents allowed fear to hold us back. I think the same can be true for parenting. Having worked with youth in professional ministry for more than four years, I find that kids who are being raised by fear-driven parents are easy to spot. In fear-driven families, it seems that everyone ultimately misses out on some of the most majestic things in life. I'm sure (from a non-parent point of view!) that it is hard to balance protection and risk in parenting. But I've noticed that fear-driven parents seem to take *full* responsibility for and control of their child's every move, exposure, interaction, etc. It seems that they forget that God is ultimately in control. He is more powerful than evil, and He calls us to be "salt and light" in the world. It's hard to be salt and light if we cloister ourselves. We're to be *in* the world, but not *of* the world. Some of the most rebellious college students I've known have come from overly restrictive and over-protective homes.

"Getting from here to there"—navigating the years of adolescence to adulthood—can seem interminably long to all involved and especially to the one journeying. At times, it can seem like the end of the journey will never come. It can also be very challenging to stay on the trail that leads to the destination.

During our hike, I remember wondering if I would be able to make it to the top. During our "lost" period, I questioned (with at least a hint of worry!) if we would ever *find* the top. It was cold and dark, and the trail markers seemed awfully far apart. Then, just when it seemed I was caving, we would suddenly pass a marker. I was amazed at how re-energizing it was to be reminded that the destination was getting closer with each step. The trail marker served to confirm with clarity that I was indeed making progress! I would eventually reach the top!

Rites of passage became like markers for our daughters on the sometimes rough, unpredictable, and long trail through adolescence. We designated four milestone birthdays—ages thirteen, sixteen, eighteen, and twenty-one—to be trail markers on their journey toward adulthood.

The goal? To encourage and remind our children at these important birthdays that it is good to be journeying together toward the summit of their childhood. This journey was preparing them for the rest of their lives, which would, by God's grace, be lived out according to His design. Our prayer was that by the time they reached the summit, they would each be firmly established in their biblical convictions, their global compassion, and their confidence and completeness in Christ. We wanted them to know that God's personal love for them was transforming them into women who would make a positive difference in this world as well as in eternity. Each trail marker would emphasize a distinctive value necessary for the journey's end goal, which was to become set-apart women.

A "rite of passage" is defined as a ritual that marks a change in a person's social or developmental status. While rites of passage were common in history, modern-day rites are scarce; however, a handful still do exist. In Jewish culture, the bar mitzvah and bat mitzvah are such rites, as is confirmation in some faith groups. "Quinceañera" parties are held in some Hispanic households, and debutante balls are not uncommon in the southern U.S. Each of these cultural celebrations combines social, familial, and spiritual dimensions, making them events of great impact. In today's culture, birthdays of significant note are most commonly celebrated with social and familial facets but seldom with any spiritual dimension.

Kari Writes

Our direction determines our destination. And our desired destination will hopefully determine our direction. Without these rite-of-passage trail markers, it can be easy to head in the wrong direction. At least two of the trail markers—age sixteen and age twenty-one—were especially significant in getting me back on track . . . or back on the "trail," to follow the metaphor. Details of those times are found later in this book but, suffice it to say, God met me in obvious ways to redirect me back to His heart during these trail marker moments.

Julie Writes

Rite-of-passage trail markers have been amazing junctures in my life. They have been markers of both memorials and hope. Each of the trail markers allowed me to stop and reflect. Those are two things I did not do often, as life happens so rapidly and crazily. At each marker, I was challenged to look to the past to see what God had been doing in my life and to look to the future to get a grasp of where I was heading. They gave great meaning to specific birthdays that could have easily just been about parties and presents.

Lisa Writes

As the second child, I always knew what rite of passage was waiting for me. Some have asked if that made it less fun or exciting. I think it was *more* fun because I could look forward to each celebration. Besides, each celebration was personalized to fit each of our unique personalities. The actual marker was consistent with my sisters', but the application was individualized.

Though the path between the trail markers was not always without roots—upon which we sometimes stumbled, tripped, and made face-plants—God seemed to use each trail marker to refocus my heart and remind me who I was and where I was headed.

Seizing the opportunity to make these special birthdays work for us, we developed the rite-of-passage trail markers for purposes of celebration and inspiration, and in some cases, re-calibration. Now, writing from the vantage of a rear view mirror, I believe they served our three daughters well as each one navigated through her adolescent years.

You may be a single parent, feeling that the deck is already stacked against you and wondering if you can pull off these rites of passage on your own. You may have kids who have already passed these chronological trail markers and have completely missed the values described in the pages ahead. You may be thinking that your teen would wonder if *you* were smoking crack if you suggested celebrating a milestone birthday in the ways suggested. You may be painfully aware that, though you had always hoped and dreamed you would have a close and healthy relationship with your adolescent, you are far from that type of relationship in real life.

We cannot change the past. What is done is done. I strongly believe, however, that God does not want us to give up or to write off our kids at any point. My prayer is that this book will give you a vision of hope for the redemptive and life-giving power of God to effect His purposes in the lives of our families. Prayerfully consider what God wants to do for you and your children in your particular circumstances. Everyone's journey is different. There is not just one way to make the hike. This book is certainly not the only way either, but there is One faithful and unchanging hike Master who sets the ultimate destination.

No hike is free from challenges: blisters, leg cramps, fatigue, shortage of water, improper gear, getting lost, bad and sometimes tumultuous weather. But determined hikers prepare for the journey, anticipating and addressing the issues. Then they can make the adjustments necessary and get on with the hike. May the same be true for you!

We invite you to join us on this journey—trail marker to trail marker—with the hope that you, too, will be inspired to keep hiking. Regardless of where you are on the trail, we want this book to give you hope.

Chapter 3
Trail Marker One:
The Thirteenth Birthday

Don't let anyone look down on you because you are young,
but set an example for the believers in speech,
in life, in love, in faith and in purity.
1 Timothy 4:12

The thirteenth birthday is a significant passage. The first of the teen birthdays, it marks the end of childhood and the beginning of adolescence. Although for many this transition takes place long before age thirteen, we proactively worked to resist the pressure of our "hurried-child" culture. Our family focused on the value of protecting childhood, so each of our daughters anticipated her thirteenth birthday as a time of "special transition."

What trail marker did our children need at this juncture of their journey? As we considered options, we worked to identify the value that was most necessary to equip them for the trail ahead—or, conversely, what would be the most severe hindrance to them if overlooked in preparation for their continued climb toward the summit.

After much prayer and thought, "purity" was the value we chose to symbolize in this rite of passage. We were convinced that our daughters would be extremely vulnerable to the dangers on the trail ahead if they were not prepared mentally, emotionally, and spiritually to resist the pervasive and distorted messages from American popular culture about sex.

The number of sexual scenes on television has nearly doubled since 1998.[1] The average teenager in America will view nearly 14,000 sexual references per year.[2] Our kids are constantly bombarded with sights and sounds from an over-sexualized society that is completely devoid of God's design. Research confirms that the younger a child is when he or she is exposed to godless beliefs about sexuality, the more vulnerable he or she is to long-term damage.

Hence, the first trail marker was inscribed the "Value of Purity." Our goal was to prepare and protect our children from the elements which would threaten their safety on the trail to the summit.

What is purity? It is that which is clean, uncontaminated, shame-free, and wholesome. It is "as it was meant to be," meaning it is the absence, or degree of absence, of anything harmful, inferior, or unwanted. It is a virtue of innocence.

While sexual purity is a significant piece of the pie, it is not the whole of purity. *"Blessed are the pure in heart, for they will see God."* (Matthew 5:8) Beyond the physical, purity also affects the heart, soul, and mind. And all of these dimensions are important to God.

This rite of passage should be set up long before your child's thirteenth birthday. Part of the preparation for this important rite of passage includes teaching your children about God's design for sexuality well before the age of thirteen. Exactly how long before should be tailored to your child's maturity.

---

1   Kaiser Family Foundation, "Sex on TV", Nov. 9, 2005, http://www.kff.org/entmedia/entmedia110905nr.cfm (accessed 2/27/08).

2   National Coalition for the Protection of Children and Families, "Sexuality, Contraception, and the Media", American Academy of Pediatrics Committee on Public Education, January 2001, http://www.nationalcoalition.org/parenting/mediastats.html (accessed 2/27/08).

In working with families for over three decades, I have observed that many parents make the mistake of waiting too long. I have witnessed that parents who miss the opportunity to be the *first* voice speaking into their child's life about sexuality will later fight to compete with the worldly voices which got there first. These voices will include peers and, certainly, the worldly media. These messages coming from the sex-sells-everything culture are replete with godless distortions and seductive deceptions. The methods and means of advertising alone render even the most protective parents incapable of screening all such influences. Adding to the pervasive sexualized culture is the early onset of puberty and corresponding awareness of one's sexuality.

Parents can ill afford to be asleep at the switch on this most important but often difficult task of conveying solid, biblical values related to God's design for purity. Truthfully and sadly, many parents are scared silent on this subject. This may be due to the fact that most of *their* parents were silent, and perhaps also in part because they feel hypocritical or ashamed about their own mistakes.

If you hiked through your adolescent and early adult years without the proper gear to protect you (a good map, the right clothes, sturdy shoes, a compass, etc.) or without the wisdom to use the proper gear you were given—and as a result experienced painful falls, injuries, and perhaps even near-death moments— *would you want your children to follow in those footsteps? Or would you want them to avoid making the mistakes you made?*

We can be silent no longer. We live in perilous times, especially in regard to sexual morality. The landscape has shifted dramatically in the past half-century. In the 1960s, five identifiable sexually transmitted diseases existed; in 2007, almost sixty can be identified. Promiscuous sexual activity has indeed become a life-or-death issue, and we as parents must break the legacy of inherited silence and speak truthfully to our children.

Though the sexual mores of our culture have dramatically declined over the past half-century, *God's design for chastity has not changed.* The sexual relationship was created by God for the marriage relationship—period. God's heart for your child is that he or she would be abstinent and sexually pure prior to marriage.[3]

Though hardly recognizable in our sexually saturated, no-holds-barred culture, purity is still a big deal to God and is part of His design for His children. He cares about our purity because it dramatically affects the way we experience life. He's concerned about the purity of our thoughts, actions, and hearts.

If we fail to proactively teach these truths to our children, the cultural tide of contempt for God's design for purity will sweep them away. And so, we chose to make the "Value of Purity" the focus of the thirteenth year rite of passage.

We were convinced that preparing our children to make wise, God-honoring choices regarding their sexuality could not be delayed. *The convictions a child internalizes in this area will affect many of the life choices he or she will make through these critical adolescent years—some of which will determine quality of life, health, and even time of death.* It cannot be overstated how important it is for us to prepare our children for this aspect of their journey, as the perils and risks are great.

At this trail marker, we paused and prepared. We celebrated and reflected on the miles hiked and carefully established what gear was needed for the trail ahead. Knowing that we could not protect our girls from everything they might encounter, and

---

3 I include "abstinent" as well as "sexually pure" because they are not synonymous. Unfortunately, many children raised in Christian homes receive little instruction regarding true chastity and eventually practice a form of modern-day Pharisaism (hypocrisy and legalism) regarding their sexuality: they place boundaries around sexual intercourse but nothing else. All other forms of sexual stimulation and involvement are practiced, and yet they consider themselves abstinent. This produces "technical virgins."

Purity is much more than technical virginity. As we understand God's design for our sexual purity, it speaks of multidimensional levels that include the body (1 Thessalonians 4:3–8), the heart (1 Timothy 5:2), the soul (2 Peter 2:11), and the mind (Matthew 5:27–28). When coupled with teaching from the Song of Solomon which repeats three times, "Do not arouse or awaken love until it so desires" (2:7; 3:5; 8:4), it seems clear that sexual stimulation is designed for the marriage covenant and no other relationship. Teaching our children these biblical boundaries when they are young can equip them to make wise relationship choices in the years ahead.

that they would need internal convictions to make wise choices when no one was looking, we committed *to prepare our children for the trail, not the trail for our children.*

The convictions we prayed that our daughters would internalize were:

1. Sexual purity is God's idea and design, not ours.

2. Therefore, God's design is the best "trail" to follow. We consistently reinforced the truth that "Sex is great; it's worth the wait."

3. Good choices in this area of purity will lead to good things, while bad choices will limit future good options. We emphasized that though grace and forgiveness are abundantly available in "emergency room triage centers," consequences such as limps, amputations, and scars are not eradicated with forgiveness.

The "Value of Purity" is reinforced or undermined in the context of the family system. As with all truth, more is caught than taught. Our actions, attitudes, and choices we make as parents have a lot to do with either equipping or stripping our children of the protective gear they will need in the area of sexual purity.

What's a Parent to Do?

We speak with so many parents who feel that protecting their children from the negative influences of culture is like trying to hold back a tidal wave, so why try? What can they really do anyway?

Actually, there is quite a lot a parent can do. Parents have a huge responsibility to create an atmosphere in the home that upholds and reinforces the "Value of Purity." Practically speaking, for us this included the following:

• We talked openly about issues related to sexuality. No question would be considered dumb. And we as parents committed to not freak out and not faint—no matter what they asked.

- We were aware of the temptations facing them from the Internet, movies, music, books, and magazines. We committed to protect them from invasive and potentially destructive forms of media. For example, we chose not to have cable television in our home. Our computer was in a very open area of our home, and we limited their access to it. We also installed a strong filtering system to protect them from accidentally going to an inappropriate site. We set guardrails around movie watching and all related media options. We worked to instill in our daughters when they were young a love for reading and discernment in choosing wholesome reading materials. We avoided having magazines in our home such as *Teen*, *Seventeen*, or *People for Teens* (to name just a few of the pop-culture magazines that carry unrealistic and toxic body-images, opposite-sex relationship advice, and materialistic messages).

- We were aware of and involved with their circle of friends, agreeing that one-on-one dating was not an option until after the age of sixteen. We influenced them to choose to avoid dating completely in high school.

- We made our home a gathering place stocked with fun things to do and great food to eat, knowing that we could control exposure and activities in our home. My husband developed a reputation for baking the "best chocolate chip cookies ever" and kept our home well-supplied with freshly baked cookies.

Lisa Writes

We would joke that our friends did not like us; rather, they liked our parents—at least, their famous Friesen cookies!

- We set guidelines regarding opposite-sex contexts that were acceptable and unacceptable, such as never having boys in their bedrooms or in the house when we weren't home.

Kari Writes

To be honest, some of the rules seemed so lame back then, but I am so thankful for them now. Their guidelines were wise. As I got older, it became clear to me: If you avoid those questionable situations, you will avoid a lot of temptation. But at the time, admittedly, I didn't think my parents were the wise ones. Fortunately, they didn't take their cues from us. They held their ground on clear, biblically driven boundaries, no matter how much attitude or whining we attempted to manipulate them with. As I reflect now, I realize that they had the "relational equity" to hold those lines because they invested so much in being relationally and spiritually connected with us. They were not rules-only (authoritarian) parents—the kind who limit their interaction with their kids to "That's the rule" and "Because I said so." They were truly invested in us.

- We taught them about emotional boundaries as well as physical boundaries. For example, we taught them to not "play married" emotionally by spending lots of time with a romantic interest on the phone, emailing, text messaging, instant messaging, and so on. In this context, I often hear, "But how do you stop love? It just happens; you can't really slow it down." I must disagree. The pace of a relationship is largely set by exposure, and limiting this exposure limits the escalation.

Lisa Writes

One of the best decisions my college boyfriend and I made was to be intentional in guarding our hearts as we dated for two years in a long-distance relationship. He was a true leader, as he took the initiative in setting specific boundaries to protect our emotional purity as well as our physical purity. We decided to limit our phone conversations to several calls a week. We chose not to say "I love you," not to talk about marriage, and not to make plans for the future. These boundaries helped pace our relationship and protected us from making promises we could not keep. Physically, we made the decision to limit

our physical contact to holding hands and brief hugs.
When our romantic relationship ended, it was still painful,
but not nearly as painful as it would have been had we been
"playing married" emotionally and/or physically for two
years.

In our work with families and parents through the years,
Paul and I have observed both lack of awareness and lack of
proactive involvement by parents regarding guideline setting
for their teens. This was highlighted by a conversation we
had with a seventeen-year-old boy after his more-than-two-
year relationship with his girlfriend ended. From a broken
home, he had very little guidance from either of his parents.
His girlfriend's parents were committed believers, and her dad
was an elder in the church. After their break-up, this young
man poured out his heart to us regarding his regrets about the
relationship and its physical intensity. He asked, "Why did her
parents let me come to their house every night? And why did
they go to bed and leave two sixteen-year-olds in the darkened
basement watching videos? Aren't parents supposed to help
their kids?"

If our children are going to understand God's design for
purity and embrace it, they need our help and active counsel.
They do not need us to trust them to be able to handle temptation
successfully. They need us to be lovingly honest and wise with
them, so they can be honest and wise with themselves.

News flash! We will not necessarily be popular with our
kids when we apply such boundaries. They will not like us
at moments when we are "the only parents who won't let us
do _____" (whatever—you fill in the blank). Our call
is to *parent* them, not to be their friend. Eventually, they will
most likely appreciate your wisely set boundaries, providing
these boundaries are set authoritatively in the context of your
parent-child relationship, rather than in a power-tripping,
authoritarian manner.

Modesty is another facet of teaching our children about
God's design for purity. This value is increasingly hard to define
in our blatantly immodest culture, and yet it is a value we must

proactively pursue. It is not okay to wear "whatever" just to fit in and not be different. I am in no way advocating an opposite extreme that also draws attention, but I am challenging parents to consider the correlation between purity and modesty.

Julie Writes

This is clutch! Dressing modestly is already a distinctively different way to dress; however, it should not be alienating. I believe that Christ calls us not to draw attention to our external appearance, whether it is being immodest or freakishly modest.

It is hard to find cute, stylish clothes that are modest, and it might take extra time and money to do so. Parents, please be willing to walk alongside and help your child live inside the guidelines you have placed around them.

I distinctly remember being *shocked* when my mom didn't flinch at spending way more than usual on a bathing suit for me because it met the one-piece standard and I liked it!! This left a *huge* impression on me. I got it! She affirmed my fashion sense, helped me grasp a bigger picture of purity, and was willing to walk the road with me.

In a recent meeting with college girls during which we were discussing this subject, one young lady asked, "Why can't we wear whatever we want? It's the guys who have the problem; if they'd get their minds out of the gutter, they wouldn't be thinking lustful thoughts and blaming it on us."

Why can't we wear whatever we want? Good question! The answer is found in the responsibility which accompanies our membership in the body of Christ. *We are daughters of the King of kings! We represent Him wherever we are!* As such, we're called to be holy, set apart. We're called to live pure and chaste lives. Further, scripture calls men to treat women "as sisters, with absolute purity" (1 Timothy 5:2). As our daughter Julie says, "How can I expect a young man to treat me with purity if I'm dressing in a way that is seductive or provocative? If I want to marry a godly man with a pure mind, I have to do my part by not becoming a stumbling block for him." Well said!

Julie Writes

Girls, let's be honest. We think very differently than guys. Like it or not, men are visually stimulated. Many of us think that if a guy can't keep his mind pure, it is his fault. We think that we shouldn't need to change our cute outfits just because guys are so weak.

Think of this from a different angle. Our brothers in Christ are striving for purity and, as sisters in Christ, we want to aid them in this. A good friend once said, "If you dress like a piece of meat, don't be surprised when a man treats you like one." Harsh and yet true. Dress in such a way that when a guy looks at you, he sees Christ shining through. Godly guys tell us this is an irresistible and beautiful quality in a woman of God.

We need to develop authentic beauty rather than skin-deep beauty. And besides, if we dress to kill and we get a guy to fall for us, it's only a matter of time before his head will be turned by another looker.

Our daughters have all said that their father has been the most important voice to them regarding modesty.

Julie Continues

When my mom told me something was immodest or inappropriate to wear outside, I'd hear it as one more command to do or not do, along with "Clean your room," "Do your homework," "Don't wear that," and so on. But when my dad talked to us about what goes through the male mind when he sees an immodestly dressed woman, we'd find it disturbing and disgusting, and we'd change immediately into turtlenecks! Not really, but it definitely opened our eyes to stuff we didn't know. Honestly, I think a lot of girls start out dressing somewhat immodestly because it's stylish and cute, but I think they continue to dress immodestly because it attracts attention.

I realize that we are bucking a powerful cultural tide when it comes to modesty and purity, but we cannot give up the battle. These values are taught to our children from the time they are young, when we teach them about their private parts and the protection due them. We taught the girls lessons in modesty long before they had anything to cover up, because we wanted them to understand the heart of modesty—which runs far deeper than skin. We did not want them to reduce the concept to legalism. We tried to teach them that it is very possible to be dressed modestly but to act immodestly. "Sexy" is the overused adjective of our times and as such bombards our children's minds constantly. We wanted to help them *think* modestly, as well as dress modestly.

Issues related to clothing can cause great tension in a family. This was certainly true in our home. To reduce the potential arguments connected with differing clothing tastes (I would have happily dressed them in Baby Gap outfits all their days!), our agreement was that *modesty* would be the only hill to die on.

Lisa Writes

Clothing was the source of much of our conflict as teens. We all wanted to fit in and look cute. Our parents worked together with us to help us understand the reasons for their rules for modesty. Because it is a biblical principle, their case was pretty airtight. As we worked it through, it was *huge* for us that our dad was so involved. It was compelling and convicting for us when he'd explain to us why and how our clothing would affect guys.

If you're a single mom, don't panic! Think of an uncle, a youth pastor, an older male cousin, or a grandpa who might be in a position to speak these truths to your daughter(s). You might even suggest to your youth pastor to lead a relationship series, a part of which might feature a panel of guys and girls who could address such issues. I've heard guys speak on this subject powerfully and effectively.

Arriving at the "Value of Purity" trail marker, we presented each of our daughters with the promise of a purity ring that would serve as a symbol of their commitment to these values—which, by the grace of God, they were fully embracing. The ring would be worn as a constant reminder of the vow made to honor God, oneself, one's future mate, and the generations to come with the "Value of Purity." Notice I wrote, "promise of a purity ring." Soon after each birthday, we chose a ring that matched that girl's uniqueness and symbolized the essence of purity. Kari's ring is a series of five hearts. The biggest heart in the center represents Jesus and His centrality to life and purity. The two hearts on each side were to represent Kari and her heritage and her future husband and his heritage (should God give her the gift of marriage—which eventually He did). After purchasing and presenting the ring, we suggested that she wear it on her left-hand ring finger as a place-holder of sorts, to be replaced by a wedding ring eventually. Lisa's ring is three bands intertwined, each of a different precious metal, representing Christ, herself, and her future spouse. Julie's has a small diamond inset in a rose-gold band with five hearts carved into the band.

If you have already chosen your child's purity ring prior to her birthday, it's appropriate to give it to her on the day. (We just weren't that together at the time!)

Each of the rite-of-passage celebrations was held in the midst of our immediate family. Our guest list also included close family friends, spanning all generations, who were significantly involved in our daughters' lives. Besides having lots of food and fun, we set aside a time for remembering significant moments from the past that ran the gamut from the funny to the sublime. That was followed by a time of blessing led by Paul. At this trail marker, the presentation of the purity ring happened privately (partly because we had not yet chosen it, and partly because we felt it was an appropriate parent-child moment).

We also marked this rite of passage with several privileges. To concretely signal the transition from childhood to their teen years, we gave them their first razors for shaving their legs and accompanied them to get their ears pierced. (These events also happened just in the circle of our immediate family.) We were acknowledging their entry into a new season of life and were closing the chapter on their young childhood.

The heart of these symbols had its roots in our diligence to protect their childhood from being rushed or hurried. We were committed to avoiding the "overexposed, underdeveloped" syndrome common to children in our sophisticated society. Although there is nothing magical about shaving legs and piercing ears, we chose these as symbols of the passage from childhood to adolescence. The point is not the specific privileges chosen; it is rather the challenge for us to consider how to resist the cultural pull on children to grow up too quickly. The reality is that American culture seems bent on robbing our children of their childhoods and consistently attacking the biblical foundation for godly, intentional trailblazing. Throughout our daughters' teen years, we felt the need to be proactive in slowing down the rush to get to the summit too soon.

Admittedly, many girls have already been shaving their legs and had their ears pierced by this point, so other more fitting symbols can be chosen for them. For example, one friend granted her child the privilege of traveling alone to visit grandparents to celebrate the thirteenth. Another transferred to her child a set amount of money for buying school clothes as of age thirteen. Some parents have permitted their children to expand their athletic competence and development by allowing them to go to a summer sports camp once the thirteenth birthday was reached. Some parents have increased computer time, bedtime, or cell phone usage. We have friends who decided that their child needed to be thirteen before going on a foreign short-term missions trip. Others decided to mark this important passage by allowing their thirteen-year-old daughter to rent a horse and assume responsibility for its care. Use your imagination! Take what you know of your child and make this passage meaningful.

And so, the first trail marker was reached. We paused there, reflecting on the delights of the previous thirteen years and on the path trod. The celebration would note the past and look toward the future. Thirteen was the beginning of a new section of the trail. The known aspects of the path ahead upon which they were about to embark were limited, but the girls were reminded that they weren't journeying alone. Rather, they were hiking with a network of people who loved them and were fully committed to them. The unknown aspects were a bit scary: Would the path be too hard? Too restrictive? Too protected? Too unprotected? Too long? Would the gear, the maps, and the supplies for the journey be adequate? Our heart's desire was to launch them on this next leg of the journey reinforced in their belief that God's design is best and that arranging their lives around God's purposes would allow them to experience His best. Embracing purity would be foundational in this goal.

If You Have Sons . . .

The trail marker, the "Value of Purity," is gender-neutral. Though a double standard has long existed in our world regarding purity, it is nonexistent in Scripture. *How can a young man keep his way pure? / By living according to your word.* (Psalm 119:9). God is as concerned about the purity of our young men as He is our young women.

How powerful it is, then, against the backdrop of low expectations, for young men to commit themselves to embracing God's call to purity! Men *can* honor God and all women by choosing the path of purity. This trail marker is critically important for them, as it will have a profound effect on all future trail markers.

A purity ring is a fitting symbol for a young man committed to abstinence. Some guys do not wear rings, in which case the ring can be worn on a chain around the neck. Having a tangible symbol of this commitment is important.

The symbols we chose for transitioning our girls from childhood to adolescence (shaving legs and piercing ears) are culture- and gender-specific. The key here is choosing something meaningful for your son that conveys the promotion to this new season of life. Remember these are privileges, not rights. Be creative in thinking of ways to symbolize this important trail marker in a way that will be positively meaningful to your child. One dad we know takes his sons on a "men's only" hunting trip once he turns thirteen. Another allows his son to get more specialized athletic training by attending a week-long sports camp at the 13th birthday.

See appendix for celebration ideas contributed by others.

Summary of Trail Marker One
The Value of Purity
The 13th Birthday

Focus ⏤

To celebrate the official passage from childhood to the teen years

Preparation ⏤

Ongoing, open, informative, and instructive talks about God's design for purity on every level: sexual, emotional, spiritual, and mental

Symbol ⏤

Presentation of a purity ring, necklace, or other appropriate representation

Privileges ⏤

For girls: shaving legs, piercing ears

For girls or guys: giving your children the privilege of managing a set amount of money to be used for clothing; establishing a Father-Daughter date night or a Father-Son once-a-month event; extending bedtime or time on the computer—or something which makes them feel like they're "growing up"

Ideas for My Teen's Trail Markers:

_____

_____

_____

_____

_____

_____

_____

_____

_____

_____

_____

_____

_____

_____

_____

_____

_____

_____

_____

_____

_____

_____

Suggested Resources

Ingram, Chip, and Tim Walker. *Sex 180: The Next Revolution*. Grand Rapids, Michigan: Baker Books, 2005.

This book challenges us to start a new sexual revolution, based on biblical truth, to counter the devastating effects and direction of the 1960s sexual revolution.

Jones, Stan and Brenna. *How and When to Tell Your Kids about Sex: A Lifelong Approach to Shaping Your Child's Sexual Character*. Rev. ed. Colorado Springs: NavPress, 2007.

This book is a very comprehensive, equipping book. They have also published an excellent four-part series on the same subject, each book age-specific.

Stenzel, Pam. *Sex Has a Price Tag*. Grand Rapids, Michigan: Zondervan/Youth Specialties, 2003.

This excellent one-hour DVD presents the potential costs of sexual activity outside of a monogamous marriage relationship. Pam is an excellent communicator and builds quite a compelling case for sexual purity. Order the DVD at www.pamstenzel.com.

Chapter 4
Trail Marker Two:
The Sixteenth Birthday

Therefore, encourage one another
and build each other up...
1 Thessalonians 5:11

Peer pressure wields great positive and negative influence and power. Many good things are set in motion by positive peer pressure (teen mission trips and "True Love Waits" conferences are two good examples of this). Many more not-so-good things are influenced by negative peer pressure and, unfortunately, it is a rare teen who is unscathed by some expression of this. Although peer pressure is usually thought of as a teenage issue, adolescents certainly don't have a corner on it. Adult peer pressure commonly expresses itself in materialism, fashion, status, social settings, and appearance management. It runs rampant across generational contexts in our culture.

Negative, adolescent peer pressure is exponentially more dangerous, however, because it influences children to make unwise decisions that can have lifelong ramifications. We are aware of far too many teens whose lives are set in a negative direction because of choices made in the context of intense peer pressure:

- Sexual experimentation resulting in unwanted pregnancies, abortions, and sexually transmitted diseases
- Debilitating injuries and sometimes death sustained from drunk driving accidents
- Brains damaged from drug and alcohol abuse
- Educational pursuits blocked because of poor performance or non-attendance in school

Our kids are vulnerable to the messages they receive from the culture and from their peers. They want to be okay by the standards of their peers; they want to belong, to fit in, to be accepted. And to some degree, we want that for them as well, providing it does not compromise who God is calling them to become.

How do we as parents affect whose voices they will value most? How do we mitigate the effect of the negative peer influences and maximize the healthy life-giving voices speaking into their lives? How do we powerfully communicate unchanging, eternal biblical truths in the midst of a pervasive, ungodly culture?

These questions and ponderings influenced our decision regarding the next trail marker. While many Americans mark the sixteenth birthday with a driver's license and sometimes a set of keys, we felt the greater need was not transportation but inspiration. As a result, the "Value of Affirmation" was inscribed on the sixteenth birthday trail marker.

At this critical rite of passage, we were compelled to shout into the life of our child all sorts of positive and affirming truths unique to her person and journey. We had noticed that our oldest daughter, Kari, was at times caught in the crossfire of peer messages and our messages. The "cool factor" was appealing to her desire to belong, and for a time, her hairstyle, fashion sense, and social desires were . . . quite honestly, a bit scary to her conservative, down-to-earth, and seemingly un-cool parents.

I recall that more than a few conflicts emerged over these issues. We desperately did not want her to become "too cool for life," a common attitude rampant in the teen world. We longed for her sense of self to be securely rooted in God's Word and His eternal values, as opposed to the passing notions of her peer group. We acknowledged that part of our concern and conflict of this season was due to healthy *differentiation* (the psychological term for the stage in which a child becomes his or her own person and adopts his or her own convictions). We felt that without our consistent, intentional prayers and our proactive involvement in her life, she was at risk for wandering off the trail with peers who clearly did not display the slightest sense of positive direction.

Kari Writes

Every child desperately wants to be assured that he or she is accepted and loved. In the teen years, we may put on the front that we don't want that affirmation, love, and acceptance from our parents, but we need it then more than ever.

We had an epiphany when we realized that our criticism of Kari's choices was not helping but hurting. Our cracking down on her with increased words of correction, spoken with the intention of redirecting her back to the path, actually had the opposite effect. Rather than closing the gap that had developed between us while communicating our disapproval of her decisions, we were driving her into the arms of her peers, who thought everything about her was great. Our disappointment, confusion, and increased feelings of failure turned to despair, as it seemed to us that we were losing her.

We didn't need to be rocket scientists to figure it out: She wanted less of our input (even though we said, "We're just trying to help you!") and more of her friends' acceptance. We also noticed that this was not just our isolated family problem. It seemed fairly common with her age group.

The journey was becoming a bit more challenging. We could see that Kari was beginning to break trail. And I'll admit we were taken by surprise. How could she want to leave the safe and carefully groomed trail we had set for her to travel? *What was she thinking?*

As we prayed about how to handle this uncharted terrain, God helped us see beyond *her* behavior to *ours*. Our own shortcomings, which were contributing to her moving away from us, came into clear focus. We came to realize that we were blurring the line between *authoritative* and *authoritarian* parenting—the former being relation- and principle-based versus the latter being heavy-handed, "because-I-said-so," parenting. Our fears of her getting lost produced behavior in us which might have ensured just that. Our attempts to correct her course through criticism had unintentionally created the exact opposite effect.

We sought counsel from some of our mentors, one of whom suggested we read *The Five Love Languages* by Gary Chapman. We had many "a-ha!" moments during our reading of this helpful book. It illuminated an important truth about Kari: "Words of affirmation" was her primary love language. She felt most loved when we encouraged her with positive, affirming words. And when she felt most loved, she would be at her best. Conversely, we discovered that words of criticism drained her "love tank" and could make her feel unloved. We have witnessed that an unloved person usually acts out in negative ways. In our misguided attempts to love and train her, we were actually driving her away.

The "Value of Affirmation" was therefore chosen as the focal point for this rite-of-passage trail marker. To symbolize this rite of passage, we decided to bombard her with positive messages from a host of important and consistent people in her life.

About two months before her sixteenth birthday, I sent requests to significant people in her life (nuclear as well as extended family members, teachers, coaches, pastors, youth leaders, and important friends—most of whom shared our faith position but also some who did not). I asked them to write her a letter of affirmation that would become a part of her "Words of Affirmation" scrapbook. I suggested that the letter could include a unique and positive character quality seen in Kari (supported by a poignant or humorous anecdote) and a blessing for her future.

Our fervent hope and prayer was that this trail marker of

affirmation would define with clarity how far and how *well* she had journeyed to this significant point in her life. Its purpose was to cause Kari to pause and positively reflect on God-given blessings and relationships while pointing her in the direction that would move her closer to the destination.

16th birthday "words of affirmation" request:

Dear Family and Friends of Kari Friesen,

As unbelievable as it may seem, in eight short weeks Kari Friesen will be sixteen. Yes, the idea is unsettling to us, but we can't argue with the calendar. She, herself, is not unsettled in the least, but rather is eagerly counting the days.

To honor her and to SHOUT into her life words of affirmation, we're inviting you to take a few moments to write a tribute to her. You may wish to reminisce about special moments you've shared with her or make an observation about her as you've watched her grow up. We'd like for you to reflect on who she is, perhaps by identifying a strong, positive character quality you see in her, and give her a blessing for her future.

Please write on only one side of a piece of pretty paper, as I will mount all submissions in a Creative Memories album. Feel free to include any photos you may have which would prompt a happy memory.

Send your entry to me as soon as possible. Her birthday is May 27, and I'll be putting the album together in the week prior to that date.

Thank you so much for your help with this special gift. I know this will be very meaningful to Kari because each of you is so meaningful to her. Many thanks in advance for your part in this gift which will keep on giving.

Gratefully,
Virginia Friesen

P. S. If you miss the date, please send it whenever you can, and I will add it as it's received. Also, if email is more your style, that works for me, too. Just send it, and I'll take care of the rest!

Soon after, the letters began pouring in, which I then put into the scrapbook. Some sent photos, some made an acrostic with her name; some wrote several pages, some a paragraph. All communicated sincere affirmations of Kari.

On her sixteenth birthday, in the presence of family and chosen family friends, we presented the scrapbook to her by reading several of the letters aloud. She was blown away. Later that night, she read each one of them, one by one, hearing loud and clear positive, life-giving messages directed personally to her. They were written by people who knew her, who were committed to her, who wanted the best for her, who believed God had some really big plans for this sixteen-year-old who had (mostly) exhibited Christlikeness, honesty, and passion throughout her life.

Today, all three of our daughters would say that their "Words of Affirmation" scrapbooks are among their most treasured possessions. Each has thumbed through the pages many times since her sixteenth birthday. The effect of these words on each daughter has been profound. People from all generations who really matter shouted into their lives, en masse, producing a megaphone-like impact which drowned out the potentially harmful messages of some of their peers.

Kari Writes

I am now 27, and I still pull out this scrapbook when I need to be reminded of who I am. I honestly couldn't select just one letter that stands out because each letter is from a significant person in my life. Whether it was from a family member, peer, or mentor, each letter means the world to me.

Lisa Writes

This book is still one of the most treasured gifts I have ever received. God has used this book to speak into my life often when I have been discouraged or lonely. It has been used to remind me of who I am, based on Whose I am.

Among this multi-generational group were several young women in their early twenties. It had become obvious to us that the girls could hear truth better from women slightly ahead of them on the journey than they could from us. We were intentional about capitalizing on this discovery. We invited women—women whom we prayed our daughters would want to become like—to come alongside our daughters as mentors. How blessed we were to have a number of women who had served on staff at the camp we directed for many years to become like part of our family. They were role models for the girls and, as such, were worth their weight in gold to us. They loved Jesus, were making wise choices to honor Him, and were cool! Our daughters could hear anything from them and seemed to hang on their every word. They served as credible voices and were used by God to communicate to the girls that staying on the trail to His heart was the best way. These were voices that mattered to Kari. And God used them to make a difference to her during a pivotal juncture of her life.

Kari Writes

Nina stands out in my mind right away. She was like a big sister to me. She was someone I was willing to hear truth from. When she spoke, I listened. I wanted to be like her when I grew up. She always had time for us girls, and I never felt like we were tagging along or were a burden to her. She was a woman who loved God and served Him in all she did. I am so grateful for her impact then and her continued influence on my life now.

To further symbolize the "Value of Affirmation," this rite of passage included the gift of a charm bracelet that would serve as a memorial of sorts. "Memorials" are spoken of in scripture as markers established to remind us of God's faithfulness and goodness. Scripture speaks of the memorial stones in Joshua 4:19–24, as reminders to current and future generations of God's faithfulness.

The charm bracelet would be representative of His affirmation of and His faithfulness to each of their unique and precious lives. The charms would be symbols reflecting God's presence in their lives. One of Kari's charms is a small figure skate, representing her passion, gifting, focus, and competence as a figure skater during her teen years. Lisa's bracelet includes a steel pan drum, representing God's work in her life during several family mission trips to Trinidad. Julie's holds a small, silver flip-flop. It symbolizes her brush with death, or at least with severe injury, while hiking along Catalina Island's rocky coastline wearing flip-flops. The incoming tide had covered the narrow shoreline with churning water, and had forced her to climb up the coastline cliff about twenty feet. The rock she had placed her weight on gave way, sending her plunging onto the rocky shore below. By God's grace and an obvious band of angels, she walked away from it with only relatively minor injuries . . . and with her broken flip-flop in hand. The little flip-flop charm reminds her that God interrupted the natural with the supernatural and that He is intimately involved in her life.

Charms are added to the bracelets year after year, imbuing them with more and more meaning. These, too, are treasured possessions.

This rite of passage also included two privileges. Though most of our culture believes that driving is the *right* of every teen, we view driving as a *privilege* and therefore not automatically determined by age. We therefore sought to discern character traits of maturity, attitude, responsibility, respect for authority, and gratitude as the girls approached the necessary age for driving. The other privilege to be earned was one-on-one dating. Just as with driving, it was not an automatic right. In fact, our hope was that the girls would choose not to exercise this privilege at age sixteen, but we felt it would "exasperate" them (Ephesians 6:4) if we told them at age twelve or thirteen that they could not date until they were age thirty-five. Kari and Lisa both broke the rule during their fourteenth year. Interestingly, at age sixteen, they chose to stick with groups as opposed to one-on-one dating. They had seen enough of their friends hurt and heartsick over struggling or failed high-school relationships, so they decided to avoid the landmines prevalent among lovesick teens. Julie wisely learned from her sisters' mistakes and avoided the whole scene altogether!

Lisa Writes

As a young teen, I felt a lot of pressure to be in a relationship and to have a boyfriend. It was hard to be the only girl (or seemingly the only girl) who did not have a boyfriend in junior high. As a high-school freshman, I transferred schools and found myself desperately trying to define who I was and what group I would be a part of. I so wanted to be liked and included that I sought to find validation through a boy. Though I was not allowed to date (I was fourteen at the time), I still thought that a boyfriend was what I needed, so I got into a relationship. Not only did I choose to deceive my parents, I also bought the lie that a relationship would validate me and would make me more complete. My entire view of the relationship was selfish and in direct opposition to what God tells me love is: *Love is patient, love is kind . . . it is not self-seeking* (1 Corinthians 13:4–5). But honestly, I couldn't see that at the time. I was just happy to feel like I was okay by peer standards.

The whole thing came crashing down when I was caught kissing this guy on school property, during school time. The worst part was that we were busted by one of my favorite teachers, which made getting caught even more humiliating. He allowed me to choose my punishment: Either tell my parents or read *Passion and Purity* by Elisabeth Elliot and write a paper on it. Because I wasn't quite ready to tell my parents, I opted for the book. In the next couple of weeks, I confessed the whole thing to my parents. They were great: grace-giving and forgiving and most concerned that I would learn what I needed to learn. Thankfully, I did, and my remaining high-school years were wonderfully free of the drama and trauma of boyfriends!

Kari Writes

I did sneak out on a Saturday afternoon date at age fourteen and, though these days we laugh about it, it was not a laughing matter at the time. The episode happened during my "too-cool-for-life" stage. When the popular, "hot" senior guy from the church youth group asked me out, I couldn't say no. After all, that was huge in my coolness rating. Fortunately for all involved, it was just a one-date deal. My parents dealt swiftly and surely with me. I got restriction for the rest of my life and no phone ever again—not really, but they did make it really clear that lying, sneaking, and defying their authority was completely unacceptable, and I had a choice to get with the program . . . or else. After the dust settled, dating didn't seem as cool or inviting as it had. I guess I got it out of my system and didn't date again until I was out of high school.

Julie Writes

It was an amazing blessing for me to have two older sisters to learn from and look up to. They taught me a lot of great things and a few not-so-great things, and sometimes I even learned from their mistakes and avoided the pitfall. When Kari and Lisa each sneaked out with a guy when they were fourteen, I was taking notes.

I remember seeing the pain it caused my parents and the pain it caused my sisters. I realized that I could avoid a lot of pain that accompanies sinful choices if I learned from the mistakes they made, and so I sailed through my fourteenth year, with no scathing broken heart.

The trail marker of words of affirmation served its purpose well. It reminded the girls that they were on the trail, heading in the right direction, and not hiking alone. It reinforced their identity as women of God and clarified their positive strengths and character qualities consistent with godly values. It identified the invaluable people who would pray for them, believe in them, love them, and stand with them along the trail.

This trail marker of affirmation confirmed their God-given gifts, which made them less vulnerable to the oftentimes distorted messages from their peers. Though words of affirmation are necessary throughout life, we are convinced that overwhelming a sixteen-year-old with such positive input will keep her hiking in the right direction and not veering far off the trail. Regardless of your child's love language, showering any child with tangible evidence of his or her value and worth at this trail marker will serve him or her well.

If You Have Sons ...

The "Value of Affirmation" also is not gender-specific. For many men, "words of affirmation" is a primary love language. Even if not, affirmation is life-giving to all. We've written many letters of affirmation for young men. The words of affirmation book may be the only way you symbolize this rite of passage.

The symbol of the charm bracelet is obviously gender-specific. What could reflect God's faithfulness symbolically for your son? Perhaps a piece of jewelry (cuff links, tie tack, belt buckle, military medal) from Grandpa's or Dad's collection, or a favorite passage of Scripture on a plaque. Use your imagination and your knowledge of what's important to your son.

See appendix for celebration ideas contributed by others.

Summary of Trail Marker Two
The Value of Affirmation
The 16th Birthday

Focus ﹏

> To affirm God's truth about your child's value, significance, and worth

Preparation ﹏

> About two months ahead of your child's sixteenth birthday, send a letter or email to the significant people in their life, including family members, teachers, youth pastors, close friends, mentors, coaches, etc., asking them to write a letter of affirmation to your child (see sample request on page 55). The letter should include some positive reflections of the child along with a blessing for their future. Arrange the letters in a scrapbook (include photos if possible).

Symbols ﹏

> For girls or guys: a scrapbook
>
> For girls: a charm bracelet with charms representing significant moments in that child's life

Privileges ﹏

> Driver's license, possible use of the family car, possibility of single dating

Ideas for My Teen's Trail Markers:

_____

_____

_____

_____

_____

_____

_____

_____

_____

_____

_____

_____

_____

_____

_____

_____

_____

_____

_____

_____

Suggested Resources

Ludy, Leslie. *Authentic Beauty: The Shaping of a Set-Apart Young Woman*. Updated and exp. ed. Portland, Oregon: Multnomah, 2007.

In this important book, Ludy builds a strong case for becoming a set-apart woman—one who chooses to live for her true King, Jesus. Ludy is refreshingly honest and candid about the temptations facing young women, especially the seduction of the worldly view of beauty.

Chapman, Gary. *The Five Love Languages of Teenagers*. Chicago: Moody Press, 2001.

This great resource helps us understand how to more effectively love our teens in ways that connect to their uniqueness. It can equip us to bridge the gap that sometimes exists between our hearts and theirs.

Gary Chapman's original *The Five Love Languages* was mentioned in this chapter because *The Five Love Languages of Teenagers* had not yet been written. I highly recommend the *"Teenagers"* edition.

Graham, Michelle. *Wanting to Be Her: Body Image Secrets Victoria Won't Tell You*. Downers Grove, Illinois: InterVarsity Press, 2005.

This relevant book challenges women to exchange the cultural lens through which they analyze their body image and beauty for a realistic, biblically driven lens.

Lewis, Robert. *Raising a Modern-Day Knight*. Carol Stream, Illinois: Tyndale House Publishers, 1999.

In this great resource for raising sons, Robert Lewis proposes a counter-cultural approach to purposefully guiding a son into manhood.

Chapter 5
Trail Marker Three:
The Eighteenth Birthday

The Word became flesh and made his dwelling among us.
We have seen his glory, the glory of the One and Only,
who came from the Father, full of grace and truth.
John 1:14

Eighteen! How did we get to this marker so quickly? Wasn't it only yesterday . . .

The milestone eighteenth birthday marks the most significant transition on the journey for most young adults—going from complete dependence on parents to a significant measure of independence. This is the moment when many young adults leave home to pursue college or a career. The young adult is positioned to hike without the constant company of parents and siblings from this point on. By God's grace and through lessons learned along the way, he or she will be ready to live life well, make wise, godly choices, and contribute positively to the world.

The previous eighteen years of hiking have been invested in preparing for this trail marker. Through successes and failures, through easy times and difficult seasons, all of life's experiences, lessons, moments, and interactions have served to shape the values and convictions which inhabit your young adult's heart. Standing at this juncture is the result of great choices as well as not-so-great choices made along the way. Surely some of the most powerful lessons in life come from experiencing the consequences of poor choices. All children will wander from the trail at some points. Our sinful nature ensures that. By God's grace, however, our children will not wander far when they realize or experience the risks of the rugged and dangerous terrain off the path.

By the time this trail marker is reached, much of your young adult's character and convictions will be shaped. He or she will soon be hiking into a world that is full of darkness and distortions, evil and sin. In these postmodern times, your young adult will be subjected to continual challenges to biblical truths and will be told on college campuses and other collegiate gathering places that there are no absolute truths and that whatever they choose to believe is truth.

The rubber sole will meet the trail at this point. If your child is hiking on the coattails of your beliefs, if biblical convictions have not become his or her own, your child will not be prepared for the terrain ahead and will most likely flounder. An exorbitantly high percentage of freshmen at Christian colleges, who have been raised in Christian homes, flail morally and spiritually that first year. Perhaps faith has not become their own. Quite possibly their parents have been content with church attendance and cooperation with family values and have not given their children any latitude for discovering the depth and breadth of their own beliefs.

The eighteenth birthday rite of passage grew out of our commitment to send prepared children into the world. Going to college with them, though fleetingly tempting at times, was not an option. Therefore, we wanted them to have the confidence that they could stand firm on their own with their convictions and beliefs outside of the safety and accountability of our constant presence. We wanted them to know what they believed and why they believed it. We also wanted them to have hearts of compassion and to be women of grace. They needed to be clear on the principle that truth and grace are partners; it would be disastrous to have one without the other. In order to stay on the trail leading to the heart of God, this pair of virtues would need to be our daughters' constant companions. Hence, the trail marker at this juncture is inscribed with the "Value of Truth and Grace."

What gear is needed for this part of the journey? Equipping a child with truth obviously doesn't happen overnight, but it has been an intentional pursuit and goal of our parenting. In our family, the importance of spending time in God's Word had been a value reinforced from the earliest days of their lives through family devotionals. As our girls became readers, personal devotionals ("devos") were introduced. God's Word would be the trail map; it would guide them toward His heart. We believe that the Scriptures are inerrant, life-giving, and hope-giving, and that knowing God is impossible without knowing His Word.

Lisa Writes

From a young age we were taught that faith is based on a personal relationship with Jesus Christ. I watched my parents, mentors, and relatives deepen their relationships with Christ through personal daily devotionals, and so that habit became part of my life as I developed my relationship with Christ. Some of my junior and senior high school youth workers were also very instrumental in encouraging the development of this spiritual commitment. In one high school Bible study small-group, we held each other accountable to having consistent "devos" by enforcing group discipline (push-ups or sit-ups) for missed quiet times.

Spiritual equipping would also come through involvement with the body of Christ, the church. Church was a priority, not a casual or legalistic activity. Selecting a church which faithfully taught biblical truth was a critical link in preparing the girls to learn to discern truth. Having college-age women mentors who worked at our summer camp contributed significantly to their growth in truth. We found that by their teen years, our girls could hear truth with more clarity when it was spoken by a twenty-one-year-old college woman than when spoken by us. They could also easily discern that these women walked their talk, which made a huge impression.

Additionally, we talked about current issues endlessly. We talked about relationships, sexual purity, homosexuality, AIDS, orphans, suffering, hypocrisy in the church, politics, apologetics, forgiveness, and whatever else in the world came up. There were no off-limits questions, and no pat answers were acceptable. It was also very clear that we as parents did not have all the answers. When stumped, we would suggest that we all do some research and return to it later. We asked them to read a variety of apologetics books by authors such as Paul Little, Lee Strobel, and Josh McDowell. (See the Suggested Resources section at end of this chapter.)

As important as truth is, parents who overlook or skimp on grace send potentially unprepared hikers into the world who are self-righteous and prideful. Grace reminds us that our salvation is not a result of our works but of God's work through the death and resurrection of Jesus. Truth without grace is harsh, but grace without truth is meaningless. *The Word became flesh and made his dwelling among us. We have seen his glory, the glory of the One and Only, who came from the Father, full of grace and truth. . . . For the law was given through Moses; grace and truth came through Jesus Christ.* (John 1:14, 17)

As with each previous trail marker, reflection and projection were crucial parts of this pause in the journey. Why were they still on the trail? One of the realities we all must deal with is that we cannot force our children to keep moving toward the heart of God. At some point, their autonomy and free will take over, and only they can decide what trail they'll follow.

Have you ever seen a "poser" hiker? It's the person at the trailhead who just bought out REI. Wearing brand-new boots and carrying a brand-new, fully equipped backpack, he is ready to attack the trail, even though he is not conditioned and has never hiked. His walk does not match his talk. He is soon left behind in the dust, an illustration of the truth that what really matters is not how you start a hike but how you complete the journey. The same is true in matters of faith. Our kids are not impressed with how their parents *start* the journey; they care about how consistently we follow our own advice. A lack of authenticity is terribly disillusioning and a great turn-off to our kids.

Why are they still hiking on the trail that leads toward God? In response to being asked what most influenced their personal pursuit of God, all three of our daughters agreed that a significant part of their continuing to hike toward the next trail marker has been the authenticity of our faith. In Julie's words, "They walked their talk. They were the same at home as they were in public. We could see Jesus at work in their lives, making them more like Him, and that gave us confidence in His reality as well as hope that He could change us." Notice they do not say, "Because our parents did it all right and made no mistakes" or "They were as close to perfection as one could hope for." Authenticity is the benchmark character quality that resonates most clearly these days. Duplicity in a parent—"Do as I say, not as I do!"—drives many children away from a personal pursuit of God. Children are not impressed that their families *look* ideal. That only teaches them appearance management. The belief that "If it *looks* right, it must *be* right" eventually breaks down. In the end, appearance management is as hollow as the mannequin in the store window.

Kari Writes

The gift my parents gave us girls for which I will never be able to thank them enough is their personal, authentic walks with Jesus. Because they were in ministry full time, we always saw them "talk the talk" at work, but what was way more important was seeing them "walk the walk" at home. I remember as a child seeing my parents reading the Word during their quiet times, and I saw my mom journaling on a regular basis. (My dad hates journaling.) These spiritual disciplines reflect their desire to have a growing, vital relationship with Jesus. One of the best gifts parents can give their children is an example of an authentic walk with Jesus. You learn by example that spending time in the Word is essential for your relationship with Him. When kids see their parents acting "Christian-like" in public but not at home, it's easy for kids to eventually walk away from the faith because of hypocrisy. I'm not suggesting that my parents were perfect. They were far from that. But they were growing and being changed by Christ, and that was so inviting to us.

Lisa Writes

Besides experiencing my parents being the same people in private as they were in public, I saw my parents deal with some hard situations with grace and truth that otherwise could've caused them to become bitter or self-righteous. Especially as we got older, they talked with us about such situations honestly and allowed us to be part of the process of working through the fallout and disillusionment that comes when ungodly things happen in the church. That reinforced our belief that ultimately only God will not fail us and that our hope must be in Him and not in people. That was a really important lesson to learn, especially before we went out in the world as young adults.

With the trail markers of purity and affirmation in our rearview mirror, the driving value of the eighteenth birthday rite of passage is truth and grace. We wanted to reinforce the importance of this pair of character values and send them on the next section of trail as those who would stand for truth in the context of grace.

What does that look like in real life? What would connect the value with practice so concretely that the girls would get it? As we considered possibilities, the musical *Les Misérables,* based on the novel by Victor Hugo, came to mind. All of us have seen the musical multiple times, securing its position as our family's favorite. We have found that each viewing impacts us more deeply with the truth of the transforming power of grace. In fact, one particular event early in the musical has become a significant influence in our choice of gift, marking this rite of passage and a higher call to pursuing God's grace and truth.

In the scene after Jean Valjean has been released from prison and finds refuge in the monastery with the Bishop, his despair and hopelessness regarding his ability to support himself as a marked ex-convict drives him to steal the Bishop's silver. When apprehended by the police and dragged back to the monastery to have the theft confirmed by the Bishop, the pivotal moment of the play unfolds. Rather than confirm Valjean's guilt, the wise and kind Bishop extends grace to him by corroborating Valjean's story that the silver had been a gift. To further his gift of grace, the Bishop presents Valjean with a pair of silver candlesticks, saying, "I can't believe you forgot these!" This moment of grace transforms Valjean, who leaves as a free man with a changed heart. From that moment on, he lives his life as a grace-giver and a difference-maker.

So compelling is this act of grace by the Bishop, we chose to symbolize the eighteenth birthday rite of passage with a pair of silver candlesticks, accompanied by this blessing: "Go out into the world as purveyors of light, and live your life marked by truth and grace." In the world, they would constantly be challenged to join the darkness, to hide their beliefs under the pressure of political correctness or "tolerance," or to let their light be extinguished. They would be tempted to compromise, to be socially acceptable, to rationalize ungodliness. These are indeed unfriendly times for those who stand for righteousness, and our heart's desire for our daughters was that they would stand for truth, not self-righteously or piously, but humbly and with grace.

Kari Writes

Les Misérables is such a powerful theatrical picture of grace. It was really meaningful to receive silver candlesticks for my eighteenth birthday rite of passage. Having the candlesticks is a constant reminder that, as a follower of Christ, I am called to extend grace to all. They are a reminder that we have all been given a chance to live a new life through the power and grace of the cross and that to live a life less than that would be such a waste.

Lisa Writes

The story of *Les Misérables* has been influential in my life, as it helped shape my understanding of practical grace and taught me that a simple act of grace can be life-changing. The story as well as the music reminds me that though grace powerfully transforms, it does not change the past. Jean Valjean must deal honestly with his past if he is to be true to the call of grace in his life. Truth and grace together are a powerful message of the play.

Julie Writes

Les Misérables has left an imprint on my heart because it shows what it means to live a life marked by truth and grace. When I am walking down the street not wanting to look a transient man in the eyes, I often am reminded of the grace that was shown to Jean Valjean as a reflection of the grace Christ has shown to me. I can never forget that I, like Valjean, am a sinner in desperate need of grace, having no means to repay the forgiveness I have been granted. *Les Mis* is a vehicle through which I can easily and naturally talk about Christ—the author of grace—with those who have seen this musical.

The silver candlesticks are a constant reminder of the call to truth and grace. At this trail marker, we also gave each of our daughters a hope chest containing a collection of "things remembered" as well as "things to come." Kari's and Lisa's hope chests were yard-sale finds, refinished lovingly by their dad, and Julie's was a family heirloom from a dear friend. Each held relics from their past: a baby blanket knitted by their late Grandma Friesen, a hand-smocked dress made by a dear aunt, a special, well-loved doll, and several of their favorite children's books. Each also contained some special China tea cups and several other grown-up gifts. In the years ahead, the hope chests have become repositories for special Christmas ornaments, collectibles, and other such keepsakes. The hope chest is an ongoing memorial of life past, present, and future.

Kari Writes

From childhood blankets and baby shoes to my wedding veil and goblets, the hope chest holds the things dearest to my heart. It is a piece of furniture that holds endless memories and treasures.

Lisa Writes

Somewhat an old-fashioned gift, the hope chest is a fitting connector of the legacy of our past and the hope for our future.

Julie Writes

I'll never forget my first look inside my hope chest on my eighteenth birthday. To open it and see tangible memories of my childhood was a remarkable experience. I think my first thought was, *Wow, I can't believe she saved these relics from my past!* It struck me how intentional my mom had been to keep some important nuggets of my childhood. Not only is it a chest of memorabilia but it is a huge chest of memories. The other thing that struck me was the smell of cedar, which took me right back to my little-girl days of opening my mom's hope chest and with child-like wonder sifting through the history contained in it. It connected me to her generation and showed me that I am not alone. I have a legacy, a history, and a future.

Pausing at this trail marker, we reaffirmed our commitment to support and pray for our daughters and to entrust them on a deeper level to Him. The hiking party would change at this juncture; our children would spend much of their time from now on hiking without us, but not without Him. And our hope and prayer was that they would choose to have Him as their constant companion.

By God's grace, our children made a personal commitment to love, serve, and follow Him, so as we sent them off to college, we prayed that they would be passionate about making a difference for eternity on their college campuses. With so much bad press and so many sobering statistics regarding lifestyle choices and beliefs of the collegiate population, it's easy to believe the lie that *no college student* can make godly, healthy choices. We wanted our children to know that, indeed, a college student *can* make godly, healthy choices. Believing this, we expressed our confidence and belief in our young adults because of our confidence in their growing relationship with Him. *The one who is in you is greater than the one who is in the world.* (1 John 4:4) It's all too easy for Christians to live as though we believe that the one in the world is greater than the One within.

As the moral decay of our culture increases and as foundational truths held throughout time and eternity are obliterated with distortions and evil, we can be tempted to hide behind fortresses of our own making. We can isolate our families to attempt to protect them from the rot of sin—perhaps forgetting that the rot is within as well as without. We can instill fear into the hearts of our children—fear of the world and all that is in it. While I certainly believe in proactively protecting our families from evil, we must wrestle with what it means to be "salt and light" in this very dark world. Those convictions may seem to be at odds with one another. Can we do both? I believe we can, by the grace of God and with wisdom from above.

Perhaps we can gain insight by turning to the Old Testament book of Nehemiah. In chapter 7, verse 3, after the wall has been rebuilt, we read: *"The gates of Jerusalem are not to be opened until the sun is hot. While the gatekeepers are still on duty, have them shut the doors and bar them. Also appoint residents of Jerusalem as guards, some at their posts and some near their own houses."*

Fear-driven parents tend to build walls without gates around their family, believing that they will be safe if nothing can get in. Unwise parents leave the gates in their walls open and thereby provide no protection. They believe that their kids will be exposed eventually anyway, so why not now? This passage from Nehemiah may provide a good model of balancing protection and exposure. The wall was built with gates that remain locked and guarded "until the sun is hot." The implication is that it is safest to venture out at high noon when the dangers are much less—or at least easier to spot. Being wise gatekeepers is one of the biggest challenges parents must contend with.

As we prepared them to walk as women of truth and grace

on the trail section fraught with godless, secular humanism (the worldview that stresses human values without reference to spirituality) and entitled narcissism (the idea that life is "all about me" and "I deserve to get everything I want"), we stressed how important it was for them to be plugged into a Christian fellowship immediately upon arriving at college. While home on a break during her first year of college, Lisa was invited by her high school alma mater to speak to the seniors on lessons learned at college. Below is what she told them.

Lisa Said

How you spend your first weekend will greatly influence how you live out your college years. That first Friday night, every organization will have welcome parties and events: sororities, fraternities, social clubs, special interest groups, and Christian groups. Wherever you go that night will set tire tracks. If you're committed to developing your relationship with the Lord while at college, go to Campus Crusade, or InterVarsity Christian Fellowship, or another campus ministry right off the bat. The sooner you get plugged into fellowship, the less vulnerable you'll be to everything else clamoring for your time.

The next big decision will be Saturday night: to party or not to party. Be clear on your convictions about drinking, drugs, and sex before you're invited to a party. It'll make it easier to say no to activities you want to avoid. Sunday morning is the final test of your first weekend; it will be very tempting to sleep in and blow off church just this once. Decide that you will get involved in a local church right from the get-go. Good churches around the college campus often provide rides to their services and are geared to the college crowd. Don't "forsake the gathering together with God's people." Sundays will be a valuable time for recalibrating your hearts with truth. The lack of that input will make you increasingly vulnerable to the distortions of the world. Besides, going to church will increase your opportunities to be invited into a real home and have a home-cooked meal!

Wise words from one so young! The college years do not have to be spent wandering in the wilderness of confusion, experimenting with all manner of evil, and making choices that could have negative effects on the rest of your life.

Believing that our set-apart kids can be part of the solution rather than the problem, we aimed to instill in our daughters responsibility on many levels. Their personal spiritual growth was one level and their intellectual expansion was another. Additionally, we wanted them to exercise responsibility connected with being citizens of our nation. We stressed to them the importance of voting as one of their civic duties. How did we do this? Primarily, we set the example to them by exercising our own right to vote. During every election, the girls watched us go to the polls and "voice" our political opinions. We also discussed current events and politics with them long before they were able to vote. When they arrived at the eighteen-year milestone, they were committed to register and vote as responsible citizens.

The eighteenth birthday trail marker is of great importance. Eighteen years under the belt . . . years covering the greatest rate of growth in life. No other eighteen-year segment of life encompasses as much change, growth, or potential. And it's in the rearview mirror now. The path ahead travels through uncharted territory. All the years of training, preparation, and development internally and externally will be tested on the open trail. By God's grace, with the trail marker of the twenty-first birthday in the not-so-distant future, your young adult will keep hiking on a trail that will lead to the summit of God's purposes for life.

If You Have Sons . . .

The trail marker, the "Value of Grace and Truth," is as critically important for young men as for young ladies. However, the symbol we used, silver candlesticks, does not cross over well—nor does the hope chest! For guys, a leather or special study Bible is a fitting symbol for the "Value of Grace and Truth." And for the hope chest gift parallel, a carpenter's belt, good fishing or hunting equipment, a tool chest, or camping or hiking equipment can represent something of lasting value that will go with your son into his adulthood.

See appendix for celebration ideas contributed by others.

Summary of Trail Marker Three
The Value of Truth and Grace
The 18th Birthday

Focus ⌒

This first real passage into adulthood celebrates internal convictions and character.

Preparation ⌒

All of life has been preparing for this passage, but our understanding of God's truth continues to deepen with time and instruction. Reading a number of books on apologetics (see Suggested Resources) is necessary preparation for your child who will soon enter the collegiate world.

Symbol ⌒

For girls: silver candlesticks (from *Les Misérables*) to represent truth and grace. We put the candlesticks in a hope chest, which also contained relics of their childhood and things for the future.

For guys: some ideas include a nice leather Bible, a carpenter's belt, good fishing or hunting equipment, a tool chest; something that fits your son's interests and that will have lasting value.

Privileges ⌒

Registering to vote, going to college (or some form of further education)

Ideas for My Teen's Trail Markers:

Suggested Resources

APOLOGETICS

Little, Paul. *Know What You Believe: Connecting Faith and Trust.* Rev. ed. Colorado Springs, Colorado: Cook Communications, 2003.

————. *Know Why You Believe.* Rev. updated ed. Downers Grove, Illinois: InterVarsity, 2000.

McDowell, Josh. *The New Evidence That Demands a Verdict: Christianity beyond a Reasonable Doubt.* Rev. updated ed. Nashville, Tennessee: Thomas Nelson, 1999.

Strobel, Lee. *The Case for Christ: A Journalist's Personal Investigation of the Evidence for Jesus.* Grand Rapids, Michigan: Zondervan, 1998.

————. *The Case for Faith: A Journalist Investigates the Toughest Objections to Christianity.* Grand Rapids, Michigan: Zondervan, 2000.

RELATIONSHIPS

Castleman, Robbie. *True Love in a World of False Hope: Sex, Romance, and Real People.* Downers Grove, Illinois: InterVarsity, 1996.

This book takes an important look at how to distinguish *true love* from the counterfeit experiences and promises of physical liaisons.

Elliot, Elisabeth. *Passion and Purity: Learning to Bring Your Love Life under Christ's Control.* 2nd ed. Grand Rapids, Michigan: Revell, 2002.

This book is a counter-cultural challenge to take a radical approach to relationships, proposing that passion and purity *can* coexist.

Friesen, Paul. *Letters to My Daughters: A dad's thoughts on a most important decision—marriage.* Bedford, Massachusetts: Home Improvement Ministries, 2006.

A collection of fifty-two letters written by Paul Friesen to his daughters, this book expresses the timeless wisdom and depth of a father's heart regarding the preparation for marriage. Though written to his daughters, the book speaks to young men as well since character qualities and convictions are the focus.

Chapter 6
Trail Marker Four:
The Twenty-First Birthday

"What good is it for a man to gain the whole world,
and yet lose or forfeit his very self?"
Luke 9:25

Delight yourself in the Lord
and He will give you the desires of your heart.
Commit your way to the Lord;
trust in Him and He will do this:
He will make your righteousness shine like the dawn,
the justice of your cause like the noonday sun.
Psalm 37:4–6

The twenty-first birthday in American culture marks the passage from adolescence into full adulthood. Because this is the official legal age for drinking in America, alcohol is often a significant part of the celebration. It is not uncommon for twenty-one-year-olds to get intoxicated as they enter adulthood with all rights and privileges. And truly, the furthest thought and intention from the mind of an inebriated person is that of making a positive difference in the world.

As young adults arrive at this highly anticipated and celebrated juncture, what trail marker might be most crucial to their life journey? What value might equip and direct them toward the future with clarity and hope? How might we as parents of a new twenty-one-year-old assist our young adult in his or her vision for the goodness of cooperating with God's will and design for his or her unique call?

After much prayer and thought, and with a determined desire to seize this milestone birthday in a meaningful way, we inscribed on this trail marker the "Value of Life Purpose." What do the words *life purpose* mean in practical terms? Simply, at its heart, life purpose is the articulation of the belief that God has created each person with a uniqueness and with a call to use his or her unique gifts to contribute something to this world and to the next. Life purpose will be uniquely fitted to each of your children, representing gifts and goals that only they can contribute.

It is well documented that most twenty-one-year-olds are relatively clueless about their purpose beyond their accustomed entitlement and self-indulgence. Though there are exceptions, the majority of our youth seem to believe that life revolves around them, and because the world around them is so messed up, they have permission to live in an Epicurean fashion: "Eat, drink, and be merry, for tomorrow may never come." As a result, hundreds of thousands of twenty-one-year-olds are wandering in a self-induced fog, with visibility limited to the next temporary high or escape. Sadly, too few of our young adults have a positive view of the potential that exists within them. How might we spur them on to impact the world positively, in a way unique to them that honors God and serves His divine purpose for their lives? Let's look at the trail marker that marks the arrival at the first summit of life.

For twenty-one years, our hiker has been on the trail. Throughout the journey, the hiker has been coached, trained, and led by parents on whom he or she has been dependent. From this trail marker forward, this child-turned-adult will assume responsibility for living life independently.

As our daughters reached the summit of their lives as

children, we wanted to reinforce and emphasize the truth that each had God-given gifts, passions, and aptitudes that when lived out would make a unique mark on this world. We believed that each one has a purpose to fulfill in this world. They were not random, they were not duplicates, and they were not unimportant. Though we had told them repeatedly throughout their lives that they were uniquely special, we wanted them to grasp with greater awareness and clarity their God-given life purpose.

People who are driven by purpose will accomplish much more and experience deeper fulfillment in life than those with no clear sense of direction. It is clear to most of us on the trail that our world does not need any more purposeless twenty-something-year-olds. Rather, as invested parents, we need to purposefully examine how to spur on our young adults to use their God-given potential to impact communities wherever they are.

Gail MacDonald was the first to teach my family and me the importance of writing a life purpose statement (LPS) through her book *Keep Climbing* (later re-titled *A Step Farther and Higher*). She so convinced us of how an LPS could have such a dramatic effect on how one lived life that I was persuaded to write my own LPS. (See end of chapter.) My articulated LPS soon became the grid through which I processed life. It impacted and clarified my day-to-day decision making, commitments, goals, and priorities. We were convinced that an LPS would be an important, practical tool for the girls to use to discover and hone their sense of purpose. So we chose to have this value be the focal point of this rite of passage.

And through this, we birthed the "Life Purpose Journey" rite of passage. We had journeyed together through the trail markers of Purity, Affirmation, and Grace and Truth; it now seemed fitting to affirm that those earlier markers served as preparation for discovering God's unique purposes for them.

Our oldest daughter Kari returned home from completing her junior year of college, just weeks before her twenty-first birthday. Awaiting her was a large envelope, sent from the "Friesen's Publisher Clearinghouse Sweepstakes." When she opened it with curiosity, she discovered that she had "won" a trip for two to Europe . . . to go on a "Life Purpose Journey." Just the thought of returning to Europe was delight enough for her, for she had spent her first year out of high school in southern Germany at a Bible school nestled on the shores of Lake Constance. The fine print of her "grand prize" further revealed that half of the trip was planned, but she could choose how to spend the balance of the journey. It was also disclosed that her traveling companion had been chosen: me!

We made the decision that I would take each of the girls on their journey for several reasons. The main objective was to have a focused, one-on-one, mother-daughter lifetime experience driven by purpose. Additionally, we wanted to imbue them with confidence that, as women, they can be competent and capable travelers. Having always had their father at the helm of all family travels, we wanted them to know that women could read maps (Bad example! Men don't read maps . . .), drive raceways (a.k.a. the Autobahn!), negotiate deals, and discover new lands. We desired that they see the world as a classroom—open to them, even as single women. Besides all that, I *love* Europe, and I longed to have this once-in-a-lifetime, mother-daughter event. Their father had had many very special and memorable daddy-daughter moments over the years, so this seemed fitting to be my entry in their journals. And though Paul did not travel with us, he was a huge part of planning, preparing, reserving, and providing for us. We could not have done it without him.

The laboratory we chose for impressing the "Value of Life Purpose" at this trail marker was the actual life journey. I took each of our daughters on a trip to Europe with a purpose. We spent 10–14 days traveling through Europe, off the beaten path, as we hiked, toured, and experienced. It's impossible to express what these journeys mean relationally. This one-on-one experience, chock-full of memorable moments, physical challenges, cross-cultural delights, culinary treats, and life lessons never to be forgotten, was unlike any other event in my life as a mother. The pictures, the journals, the scrapbooks all fall short of capturing the intangibles of these wonderful journeys. Each was a time of learning—about one another, about God, about life. Together we encountered and learned about the world at large through the eyes of other cultures. We enjoyed indulgences such as taking the *Jungfraubahn* to the "Top of Europe" and found delight in the practice of frugality by staying in hostels and going to grocery stores rather than eating all meals out. We practiced perseverance (more my lesson than theirs) as we hiked well beyond my level of comfort. We intentionally slowed down to smell the roses and see God's creativity in a foreign context. This often required us to adjust expectations when necessary and to "give thanks in all circumstances" (1 Thessalonians 5:18).

Kari Writes

This trip was one of the most amazing experiences of my life. I would recommend it a million times over. Experiencing God's creation, different cultures, and the life lessons learned while traveling are invaluable!

Lisa Writes

This rite of passage was absolutely amazing! Europe is full of beauty and examples of God's majesty. We were able to experience it firsthand as we slowed down and adventured together. My trip happened right after I graduated from college. I was at a turning point, trying to figure out where God was leading me for the next phase of my life. I lacked clear direction, and God used this trip to help clarify things about myself and about Him that eventually led me to understand where He wanted me. Besides, the trip was a blast, and I loved being with my mom on such an adventure.

One of my favorite memories was the night we spent sleeping in Manarola, one of the quaint and picturesque towns of the Cinque Terre. We negotiated to rent a room from "Pedro and Maria" and ended up sleeping in their wine cellar the night before we went to Florence, Italy. We had a blast, sleeping in a makeshift bed in an unfinished basement, surrounded by aging bottles filled with homemade wine. Another unforgettable memory was the "scenic tour" we enjoyed hiking the Schilthorn (the "shortcut" which extended our adventure by two hours).

Julie Writes

This journey is one I will never forget. It is filled with so many incredible memories! I felt so loved and cared for during the entire journey, and my mom and I had the time of our lives. We hiked endlessly and saw some of the most beautiful parts of God's creation. We loved immersing ourselves in the culture, respecting cultural traditions, and eating great food and gelato. More importantly, I was challenged to think about who I am and what I am about. The writing of my life purpose statement began on that journey. One of the things I realized then was that I wanted to be doing these kinds of things with my twenty-one-year-old daughter one day. It made me consider what decisions I needed to be making, so that I would continue to develop into the woman Christ wants me to be. My life purpose statement is yet to be fully finished . . . but this adventure helped me focus on life in a different way.

Ours is not the only prescribed method of success. Maybe you are a single parent and your options are more limited than ours. Perhaps the thought of going to Europe is terrifying to you or completely beyond your financial means (though I must say we traveled very inexpensively!). Custom design a journey that fits with your resources, family configuration, and passions. The goal is not the trip itself but the meaning of the journey.

Three weeks after Kari received her surprise "Friesen's Publisher Clearinghouse Sweepstakes" envelope, we departed for Munich, Germany, which was the most reasonably priced destination at that time. As we commenced the journey, I presented her with a copy of Gail MacDonald's book, now titled *A Step Farther and Higher*, along with a new journal. I had only two instructions for her: first, read at least the chapter from Gail's book on writing a life purpose statement; and second, keep a journal of our trip. Besides chronicling our travels, my goal for her was to note life lessons experienced along the way, both good and bad ones. Most importantly, I encouraged her to note moments of increased awareness of "God sightings" (moments when the presence and power of God were unmistakably seen) and to reflect on the impact of those times.

And so the adventure began. Driving on the Autobahn for the first time was terrifying initially, but I quickly adjusted. Our first stop was at Bodenseehof, where Kari was thrilled to reconnect with some important mentors from her year at this German-based Capernwray Bible School. After a memorable visit there, we forged on to Switzerland: Zurich, Lucerne, and Interlaken. We hiked the Lauterbrunnen Valley up to Gimmelwald and Gimmeln, through lush valleys, and up mountains along the *wanderwegs*. I had intentionally planned this part of the journey to take us off the beaten path.

One of life's most important lessons is that, though God is certainly present and active in our frenetically paced life, He can more easily have our full attention when worldly distractions are removed. The reality of God is palpable when we get away from our familiar life contexts and are immersed in the majesty and beauty of His handiwork. It is in moments and places such as these that we can hear the still, small voice of God which is so commonly drowned out by the noisiness of our culture.

It was in the midst of the matchless grandeur of the Swiss Alps that God met Kari in a life-changing way. She had been struggling to stay on the trail at that point in her life. Just months earlier, our family had experienced a catastrophic and horrifying loss when an extended family member had committed suicide. Bipolar disease was the framework of this precious twenty-four-year-old's life and death, which left Kari with many questions about God. *How could He allow this to happen? Why did she have bipolar illness? How is He good when tragedies like this occur?* Quite honestly, I did not know how extensively Kari's confusion and hurt had shaken her confidence in God. She had sought counseling on campus in the months preceding, so we knew she was struggling, but it was not until this moment during her rite-of-passage journey that she was able to articulate the depth of her angst.

Kari Writes

There we were—Mom and me—surrounded by the snow-topped Swiss Alps. I've never seen such beauty. Suddenly I was overwhelmed with the presence of God,

and I sensed my own foolishness at having shaken my fist
at Him. It was a transforming moment for me. I sensed
Him beckoning me back into His arms, assuring me that if
I took that leap of faith, He would catch me. In an instant,
the battle was over. I took the leap and knew I was settled
back in the heart of God, confident of His goodness, His
faithfulness, His trustworthiness. I was aware that though
I'd never understand everything about my cousin's death
or many other things that might happen in life, my faith
was rightly placed in the personal Lord of the universe, the
Hope of the world.

While that was certainly the most important life lesson
of Kari's journey, there were many more over the course of
the next eight days. The moments of delight far outweighed
the moments of frustration, but some of our (now) funniest
memories were spawned from exasperating events when things
did not go as planned. We got very lost at least twice, in the dark
of the night, and Kari was treated to seeing me melt down in
tears long enough to vent my frustration and then get a grip.

We found it challenging to understand the changing
currency from country to country (this was pre-Euros). We
were confounded by signs written in languages or symbols
unintelligible to us. And in a "this isn't how I planned it"
moment, we spent the last night of our trip in the Munich
airport. Fully expecting to easily find a hotel room near the
airport (after all, it was May—low tourist season in Europe),
we were surprised and dismayed to find that an international
trade show had filled all the hotel rooms within about 90 miles
of Munich. After wildly persisting in tracking down a room,
including stopping in many small towns in pursuit of a *Zimmer*
(a common European custom, a *Zimmer* is a room for rent in
a private home), I recognized that before us was a potential
"lemonade" moment. We could ruin our last night by sucking
on a bitter lemon, or we could "make lemonade." I must admit
in all honesty that lemonade making is a process. It took me
a while before I pulled out the "juicer," during which time
I cried, prayed, demanded, and pursued alternatives to no avail.
Once I accepted the reality that *there were no rooms in any inns,*

we settled into a leisurely, late dinner, freshened up at a rest area on our way to the airport, turned in our rental car at 2 a.m., and curled up on not-so-soft wooden benches-turned-beds in the airport. Conveniently, we were wakened early enough to have coffee and *Brezelrolls* for breakfast, and we didn't even have to leave the area to get it! We also laughed a lot about the previous twelve hours before boarding the plane for home. We gleaned another really important lesson for the trail: Life is ten percent circumstances, ninety percent attitude!

Kari and I journaled endlessly on our journey, processing God sightings and life lessons that we experienced in abundance. We learned so much about God, about ourselves, and about our relationship. We learned that He's in the small things as well as the large. We were reminded that He is faithful when things went our way and when they didn't.

By the end of the trip, we had lots of pictures, many pages of reflection, and a profound sense of having been met by God. These insights would contribute to Kari's LPS.

Writing an LPS is a process. I did not expect the girls to write their LPSs while on the trip. My goal was simply to introduce them to the concept of a LPS, so they would begin thinking about life through that paradigm. Most of all, we desired that they would continue to discover God's purposes for their lives.

What is the point of a Life Purpose Statement, and how do I write one?

A life purpose statement (LPS) becomes a focal point through which all of life's decisions are viewed. It reflects one's gifts, interests, passions, temperament, sense of call, and experiences. It is shaped by previous successes as well as failures. It recalibrates one's heart and mind in a way that helps facilitate living out one's God-ordained purpose.

An LPS is not about setting goals or making plans, though it becomes instrumental in approaching those two important strategies. Rather, it establishes a point on the horizon for which to aim. "If you aim at nothing, you'll surely hit it," says the adage. Having an LPS beckons me to look beyond today toward an unfolding future, full of potential for becoming all that God has designed me to become. It is life-giving indeed to live with the awareness that God is so personally involved in my fulfilling the purposes for which He designed my life!

As our daughters reached this summit, they looked into a bright future full of hope. This journey reinforced their sense of value and their sense of God-ordained destiny. Their LPSs equipped them with an invaluable tool that would be used to help them accomplish God's unique life plans and purposes.

Writing an LPS is not an afternoon exercise. You begin its formation by taking notes on thoughtful reflections of your passions, gifts, and experiences. You consider those things that are unique about yourself. You may identify someone whose life inspires you and resonates with your own life who will serve as a model for your LPS. Over time, you will assimilate the information you've gathered about yourself and synthesize it into a statement that will provide direction for your life.

Though there is much more of life to live and other summits to be scaled, reaching the twenty-first birthday trail marker in good stead was an answer to years of prayers, as we diligently parented from our knees in prayer. We humbly realized that reaching this summit did not mean that we had arrived at the end but, rather, that we were standing at the beginning of the rest of their lives.

Some Life Purpose Statements

Gail MacDonald, who tutored me on the importance of living by one's life purpose statement, shares hers:

I purpose, through the power of Christ within, to follow the example of Mary of Bethany who chose to set moods, be sensitive, and love sacrificially. Fully aware that my own growth is in process, taking a lifetime, I will live patiently, relax, and enjoy the journey.

Gail writes, "The purpose statement became my flag. Morning after morning, I would read it, affirm its grip upon my being, and then, in light of it, set out to write my lists of things to do that day, always asking how this or that item contributed to my sense of purpose." (*Keep Climbing*, page 34)

~

My LPS was written around 1987, when the girls were 2, 4, and 7. I wrote and rewrote it in the front of each of my journals where it would be conveniently seen most days.

I purpose to:

1. *Seek God with an open, teachable, humble heart—fully integrated and authentic in all areas of my life.*
2. *Cultivate a sanctuary of peace, grace, and truth for Paul, Kari, Lisa, and Julie first—and then for the "angels unaware" and others who might come our way.*
3. *Develop and use my gifts of hospitality, counseling, writing, and creating as doors open to "the highest and best use."*

~

Lisa Writes

I purpose to live a life that is authentic and humble as I seek to glorify God by being a woman who seeks truth and extends grace; by creating atmospheres of love and acceptance; and by bringing physical and spiritual health as I serve my neighbor.

Julie Writes

I purpose to:

1. Live in an authentic, approachable manner, exhibiting the love and acceptance of Christ to everyone I meet.
2. Live a passion-filled, peace-yielding, adventure-seeking life, using my love for the outdoors, sports, and health to bring knowledge and education to those who may be lacking resources.
3. Live each day denying myself and my selfish motives, taking up Christ's cross of love and sacrifice.

~

Linda S. Anderson, founder of Mom to Mom Ministries (www.momtomom.org), drew this diagram to represent her purpose as a parent:

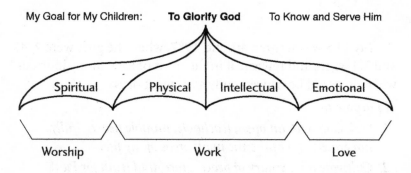

My Goal for My Children: **To Glorify God** To Know and Serve Him

Spiritual Physical Intellectual Emotional

Worship Work Love

If You Have Sons . . .

The specifics of this rite-of-passage journey should be tailored to your situation, resources, and desires. Both parents, the opposite-sex parent, or the same-sex parent can make the journey with the young adult. The trip can be anything meaningful and doable for your family, in your own country or beyond. Don't lose the meaning of trail markers in the trip. The trip is not just an excuse for a fun getaway, although it should be a lot of fun! Buy your son a manly journal and a copy of Crawford Loritts' book *A Passionate Commitment*. Remind him that his life purpose will prepare him for eternity.

See appendix for celebration ideas contributed by others.

Summary of Trail Marker Four
The Value of Life Purpose
The 21st Birthday

Focus ⁓

Confirming your child's sense of God-ordained purpose, which is unique to them. *You knit me together in my mother's womb; I praise you because I am fearfully and wonderfully made . . .* (Psalm 139:13–14)

Preparation ⁓

Again, we've been working towards this trail marker all along, but some specific helps include doing the "Myers-Briggs Type Indicator" or some form of temperament inventory with your child (*Please Understand Me* by Keirsey and Bates has an inventory included in the book); doing a spiritual gifts inventory; helping them to begin thinking in terms of "life purpose" by paying attention to their strengths and weaknesses, their passions, goals, etc.

Symbol ⁓

A journey of some sort; we've chosen hiking in Europe, equipped with backpacks, a fresh journal, and a guide to developing a Life Purpose Statement. The journal should contain a record of the journey, noting life lessons observed or learned along the way as well as "God sightings." Spend as much time as possible on the journey "being" rather than doing.

Privilege ⁓

A rite of passage journey with a parent.

Ideas for My Teen's Trail Markers:

Suggested Resources

Eldredge, John and Staci. *Captivating: Unveiling the Mystery of a Woman's Soul.* Nashville, Tennessee: Thomas Nelson, 2007.

This book takes an important look at biblical femininity and the gifts and challenges of being a woman of God.

Eldredge, John. *Wild at Heart: Discovering the Secret of a Man's Soul.* New ed. Nashville, Tennessee: Thomas Nelson, 2006.

This book takes an important look at biblical masculinity and the gifts and challenges of being a man of God.

Friesen, Paul A. *So You Want to Marry My Daughter? The top 10 questions every dad should ask and every young man should be prepared to answer before engagement (way before!)* Bedford, Massachusetts: Home Improvement Ministries, 2007.

In his humorous yet profound way, Paul Friesen asks penetrating questions that each prospective groom and bride should consider long before deciding to marry. Biblically driven and very practical, this is a must-read for all considering marriage.

Heald, Cynthia. *A Woman's Journey to the Heart of God.* Nashville, Tennessee: Thomas Nelson, 2000.

This book is a great primer on disciplines needed for the journey to Christlikeness. Anything by Cynthia Heald is worth the read!

Keirsey, David, and Bates, Katherine. *Please Understand Me.* Third ed. Del Mar, California: Prometheus Nemesis Book Company, 1984.

Using the Myers-Briggs Type Indicator as a springboard, this book contains Keirsey's own temperament sorter, which is the starting point of understanding one's temperament or "preferred operating system." This information can give insight into the reasons why one does, acts, thinks, plans, and perceives in certain ways, increasing personal understanding of how to maximize one's life potential.

Loritts, Crawford. *A Passionate Commitment*. Chicago: Moody Publishers, 1996.

Loritts challenges the reader not to settle for a life that lacks purpose, fulfillment, and vitality. He encourages pursuing one's God-given call, which is usually found in the heart of one's passion, and embracing it fully.

MacDonald, Gail. *A Step Farther and Higher: Some Turn Back, Others Never Will.* Portland, Oregon: Multnomah, 1993.

This book is out of print, but it can be located on a used-book Web site. It is also found under the title *Keep Climbing*. It is an excellent book on many topics related to the life of a disciple, and it's especially helpful on the subject of writing a life purpose statement.

Epilogue

"For I know the plans I have for you," declares the Lord,
"plans to prosper you and not harm you,
plans to give you a hope and a future."
Jeremiah 29:11

The twenty-first birthday rite-of-passage trail marker was reached. No one could have prepared us for the view from this vantage. As we looked back, we marveled that we had covered so much territory and that it had gone so quickly. (I know that is hard to believe if you are in the throes of tough trailblazing, but I promise you it is true!) Reflective thoughts ranged from some regrets as catastrophic moments resurfaced, to great joy as we delighted in recounting memory-making moments. The trail had had many unexpected twists and turns along the way, and yet, by God's grace, we had made it—together. The vista before us was expansive and full of hope and promise. Best of all, we would continue the journey, now side-by-side, as friends, joined by both DNA and choice.

The trail markers each served to emphasize the values of "Purity," "Affirmation," "Truth and Grace," and "Life Purpose." Together with intentional character training throughout their lives, these trail markers have well positioned the girls to keep journeying toward the next juncture of their life journey. Each marker attained served to reinforce that it was indeed good, indeed best, to be on the trail which by God's grace would lead them to His heart.

For that is the ultimate Destination.

Appendix

Contributions for Trail Marker One
The Value of Purity
The 13th Birthday

One of my dear friends, Jan, submits this idea which she and her husband did with their two sons:

To affirm the goodness of choosing purity, we gave each of our sons a necklace with a silver heart charm that was engraved: "Philip loves _____" or "Daniel loves _____". The intention is that when they are ready to "give their heart away," they will engrave the girl's name on the heart and present it to her, with the history that they were given the heart by their parents to save until they met the woman they would choose to spend the rest of their life with. We also gave them this letter:

Dear Son,

The time has come for us to do something tangible to let you know of our commitment to you. I think you know we are committed to praying for you for the rest of your life. However, until you discover God's choice for your life partner, we are committed to pray specifically that you will remain pure in mind, body, and heart. The greatest desire we have for all our children is that they know the Lord Jesus and desire to please Him above all else.

Secondly, we are praying that you will choose a godly spouse with whom you can share the blessings and heartaches of life. To that end we are praying for a healthy, life-long marriage that will bring the greatest joy and sense of fulfillment you can ever imagine. You already know that the freedom and innocence of living a life of sexual purity can never be bought or regained. We are so proud of the commitment you have made to enter marriage without guilt or comparison in order to experience the best God has for you. God promises to protect you, provide for you, and bless you abundantly because of your obedience to Him. We are thankful for your choice and for His faithfulness!

We will be praying for you over the years until one day you give your heart (and this engraved necklace) to the woman you choose to spend the rest of your life with. We can't wait to meet her and look forward to her becoming a part of our family. We love you and will never stop praying for you.

—Mom and Dad

Our dear friends Gordon and Barbara Becker share the Blessing Ceremony they did for their son Kyle:

When Kyle turned 12 (the same age as Jesus was when he stayed behind in the temple), we had a "Blessing Ceremony" for him to mark his first steps into manhood and to reinforce how special and unique he is to God and to us. The ceremony included affirming him, challenging him, and confirming his call to be a set-apart man of God.

This blessing ceremony was attended by family and friends, who were invited to also bless him with written and/or spoken blessings.

We chose to present Kyle with several gifts that would symbolize our hopes and prayers for his future. Many of these ideas came from the book *Celebrations of Faith* by Randy and Lisa Wilson.

- Leather Portfolio—Contains "important lessons of manhood" including Biblical principles of character and convictions that befit a man of God.

- Crest—An engraved crest with pictures that symbolize character traits that he has demonstrated in his life:
  Christ-Protected (Ephesians 6:10–18)
  Kingdom-Minded (Matthew 6:33)
  Servant-Hearted (Matthew 20:20–28)
  Compassion-Motivated—as modeled by Jesus Himself

- Cross Necklace—A reminder of what Christ did on the cross, that He died for you and because of this you can now have a direct relationship with God the father, as Jesus paid the price of your sin.

- William Wallace Sword—A replica of the original, on which we had engraved on one side these words from William Wallace: "Men follow courage, not titles" and on the other side: "Fight the good fight" (1 Timothy 1:18).

- Bible—We had bought Bibles early in our marriage with the intention to use them and then to pass them on to our children as part of their spiritual heritage. Gordon gave Kyle his, in which he had written notes about things he had learned along the way.

- Handkerchief—An heirloom embroidered handkerchief from his great-grandmother given as a reminder to pray for that special woman that God has yet to reveal to Kyle. Barbara will present the handkerchief to Kyle's wife on their wedding day.

- Scrapbook—On the spine of the album was engraved "Celebration of Manhood" and on the cover, the verse "For I know the plans I have for you . . . plans to give you hope and a future" (Jeremiah 29:11). Inside the album, we had a collection of pictures, beginning with his first ultrasound and going up to the present, that pointed to God's hand working throughout his life. The journaling included Scripture passages and words from family and significant friends who have mentored Kyle over the years.

Contributions for Trail Marker Two

The Value of Affirmation

The 16th Birthday

Gordon and Barbara Becker share what they did for Kyle when he entered high school:

We continued blessing Kyle by organizing a canoeing and camping trip for a close circle of Kyle's friends and their fathers. Gordon sent an email to a select group explaining:

> I've been thinking that I want to be intentional about continuing to develop my relationship with Kyle and to help him navigate through adolescence. I also want to develop a community of people he can count on at any time in life and who can count on him as well. These are not original ideas—just thoughts inspired from Robert Lewis' book *Raising a Modern-Day Knight*. I thought, with your help, that we could all be in this together to reach this goal for our own relationships with our sons.

The email invited these fathers and sons to go on a four-day trip. We decided to use the services of a Christian river-guide company in Maine to plan and guide the trip, believing this would enable the dads to spend more time with their sons and have far less stress in planning the trip.

I (Gordon) asked each father to prepare a devotional to share after either breakfast or dinner. The devotionals helped set the tone for the trip and focused on different challenges for fathers and sons. (Resources: *Raising a Modern-Day Knight* video series, Armor Up devotionals)

After three days of navigating the beautiful St. Croix River and sharing many memorable moments bonding as fathers and sons, we held our blessing ceremony. The purpose was to affirm and challenge the boys. I briefly explained why we were together and that we dads wanted to take some time to affirm the boys. Each dad took turns to publicly recognize each young man's strength of character. We had been around each other's sons long enough to be able to do this authentically, and it was profound for each young man to hear affirmation from another father. I then designated a time for each father/son pair to share with each other in private. Each father shared with his son his blessing and affirmation. (I asked the dads to prepare this several months in advance.) After some time, we gathered around the campfire again, and the fathers publicly committed as a group to be available to their sons, to be their "river guides" as they navigate the "river of adolescence" and to influence their growth as godly young men.

We concluded the ceremony by giving the boys two symbols that would commemorate the trip. Each dad presented his son with an engraved compass. The compass was inscribed with the definition of a godly man as well as the theme verse of the trip, *Let the wise listen and add to their learning, and let the discerning get guidance* (Proverbs 1:5). I explained that the compass is a tool that gives a traveler direction, especially if he is lost, but more often it is used to guide him on a journey.

The second gift was a personalized, leather, pocket-sized Bible—God's compass—to provide guidance and direction to travelers in life. We reminded the boys to use it to grow, to add to their learning, to get guidance, to know the heart of God, and to share it with those who are lost.

~

The Beckers also performed a blessing ceremony for their daughter Cassandra, in celebration of her sixteenth birthday:

To mark our daughter's journey as a set-apart woman of God, we invited family and significant friends to a blessing and affirmation ceremony. We asked the guests to write words of affirmation and encouragement to be shared at the ceremony and then later preserved in her photo scrapbook.

We wanted to bless Cassandra in the presence of her family and friends, to affirm her and the decisions she had made, and will make, to be a set-apart woman of God. We were also asking our family and friends to pledge to stand behind her and encourage her on her walk to become a noble woman of faith.

We commemorated the day with several symbols and gifts that we felt would remind Cassandra of, and guide her toward, God's plan for her life, including, among others:

- Purity Necklace—A sterling silver necklace with the following special charms as symbols of purity:

    Lock and a Key—Gordon took the key as a symbol of his desire to guard her purity now and will present the key to her husband on their wedding day.

    Silver Heart—This charm symbolizes guarding her heart to be pure emotionally and not to be quick to give her heart away before the right man is revealed to her by God.

    A Mustard Seed—This charm encourages Cassandra to keep pure in her faith.

    Silver Envelope—This charm represents two letters we've asked her to write: one to her future husband and one to her future children, expressing her commitment to live a pure and godly life.

    Silver Baby Shoe—This charm reminds Cassandra of her promise to be pure for the next generation. She will give the charm to her first baby.

- Alabaster Box—In the Hebrew tradition, the fathers of young maidens saved up about a year's salary to purchase an alabaster box and fill it with fragrant oil. When a maiden's future husband was accepted into the family, she broke her alabaster box at his feet. In this box, we placed a tiny vial of oil along with a letter that I (Barbara) will write to Cassandra's future husband. This letter will bestow honor and blessing upon our future son-in-law and will tell him of our years of prayers for him.

- Heirloom Etching on Wood of a Woman with a Flower in Her Hair—Barbara gave this to Cassandra as a reminder that being a woman created by God is a great privilege. The gift of femininity is something we can give both to ourselves and to people around us.

Cassandra loves to wear flowers in her hair, so this gift was very appropriate for her. She loves to be surrounded by beauty and makes her environment inviting.

Your beauty should not come from outward adornment, such as braided hair and the wearing of gold jewelry and fine clothes. Instead, it should be that of your inner self, the unfading beauty of a gentle and quiet spirit, which is of great worth in God's sight. For this is the way the holy women of the past who put their hope in God used to make themselves beautiful. (1 Peter 3:3–5)

- Princess Teacup—We gave to Cassandra this family heirloom from Barbara's grandmother as part of a tradition of special memories passed down through the generations, reminding her that she has a heritage of God-honoring women in her lineage.

- Pink Leather Bible—When Cassandra was very young, we bought a Bible for Barbara to use with the intention of presenting it to Cassandra one day. The Bible represents the need for her to be grounded in the truth. *Your word is a lamp to my feet and a light for my path.* (Psalm 119:105)

~

Another way to do a "Words of Affirmation" scrapbook, contributed by my friend Robin Kraning, mother of six sons:

We invite our extended family and families of those who have been involved in our son's growing up years (Sunday School teachers, AWANA leaders, youth leaders, school teachers, mentors, and coaches) for a "potluck dessert" to celebrate the particular son's life. We ask that they bring with them a letter of affirmation written to that son, and at the celebration, they place their letters in a scrapbook we provide. We have stickers, adhesives, and other tools necessary for posting the letter. We also take a photo of our son with each family member or friend to place on the page with the letter. After dessert, we gather and invite any who wish to, to share a memory about the birthday boy. Some share a funny story, a thoughtful act, character qualities they have observed, an accomplishment . . . It's a rich time of encouragement for the young man.

After sharing, we have a time of prayer. It has truly been amazing to see the impact of this time on our sons. They feel encouraged, empowered, and embraced by people very important to them.

~

An "online" suggestion for "Words of Affirmation," contributed by my friends Guy and Barbara Steele:

We built an "online" affirmation webpage for our son. After setting up a special site including a collage of fun photos from throughout our son's life, we secretly emailed friends and relatives ahead of time, sent them a link to the webpage, and invited them to post greetings, affirmations, and Happy Birthday wishes in honor of our son. We surprised him on the day of his birthday by showing him the website, at which many posts had already been collected. More such postings arrived in the days following, and our son enjoyed checking in every so often to visit the page and read the new submissions.

Contributions for Trail Marker Three

The Value of Truth and Grace

The 18th Birthday

My friend Robin Kraning, a mother of six boys, highlights Trail Marker Three in this way:

At age eighteen, we gather the men of our extended family, plus Mom, to celebrate the beginning of manhood. We all go out to dinner and then gather at a home to share as men (and Mom). Each comes prepared with a letter for our son. The letter is written with observations about our son and thoughts they wish someone would have told them at age eighteen. They include an encouragement and a blessing for their future. We end the evening praying for our son: his future, his school, his future mate, and for godly character and choices to continue to develop in his life.

Finally, we read a letter and have all the men sign it in the presence of our son. It begins with Colossians 1:9–14 and represents their commitment to pray for and encourage our son as he begins this new chapter in his life:

Robert Kory Kraning

". . . For this reason, since the day we heard about you, we have not stopped praying for you and asking God to fill you with the knowledge of his will through all spiritual wisdom and understanding. And we pray this in order that you may live a life worthy of the Lord and may please him in every way: bearing fruit in every good work, growing in the knowledge of God, being strengthened with all power according to his glorious might so that you may have great endurance and patience, and joyfully giving thanks to the Father, who has qualified you to share in the inheritance of the saints in the kingdom of light. For he has rescued us from the dominion of darkness and brought us into the kingdom of the Son he loves, in whom we have redemption, the forgiveness of sins." (Colossians 1:9–14)

We hereby make this covenant to *pray* for you as Paul prayed for Timothy, that God's hand would rest mightily upon you and that His grace would see you through your college years and into the future He holds for You!

This symbolizes a new relationship as men with our son for accountability and encouragement in his journey that lies ahead. It's a wonderful evening and support to our years of training to this point. It has been exciting to see our older sons transition into the role of giving input into the lives of their younger brothers.

We truly know we have been uniquely blessed with godly men in our extended family. If this were not the case, this gathering could be made up of other godly male mentors who had been an influence in our sons' lives.

Contributions for Trail Marker Four

The Value of Life Purpose

The 21st Birthday

Again drawing from the experiences of Kent and Robin Kraning, parents of six sons:

At age twenty-one, we have an extended-family dinner, and we present our son with a family ring. This ring has a family crest that we designed based on the values we sought to instill in our children since they were young. The imagery on the ring includes a sword that symbolizes our desire for them to be strong men of character, a pitcher and towel representing servanthood, and a cross as a reminder of their godly heritage and personal faith. Surrounding the images are words in Latin that mean: "Strong Faithful Servant—Walk Worthy." Our prayer is that the ring will be a constant reminder to be godly men of integrity in a world of compromise.

About the Author

Dr. Virginia Friesen has spent her life partnering in ministry with Paul, her husband since April 24, 1976. They have served on staff with InterVarsity Christian Fellowship, primarily with its family camp ministry through Campus by the Sea, IVCF's rustic training center on Catalina Island, and on staff at Grace Chapel in Lexington, Massachusetts. They are founders and directors of Home Improvement Ministries (www.HIMweb.org) and spend much of their time (when they're not hiking) speaking at marriage and family conferences, counseling, and writing. Virginia received her Doctor of Ministry in Marriage and Family Therapy from Gordon-Conwell Theological Seminary.

"The Friesen Girls" all live in California currently. Kari married Gabriel Garcia in 2007, and together they serve in youth and college ministry at Bayside of South Sacramento. Lisa works full time as an athletic trainer and continues to spend her summers serving at Campus by the Sea on family camp staff. Julie recently graduated from California Polytechnic University at San Luis Obispo and is working as a Physical Therapy aide, preparing for grad school. Virginia considers her daughters three of her best friends and they love being together, whether sipping tea in a tea room or hiking a new mountain. Best of all, they share a passion for following and serving Christ, especially in the context of marriage and family.

Virginia highly recommends her two favorite books: *Letters to My Daughters: A dad's thoughts on a most important decision—marriage* and *So You Want to Marry my Daughter? The top 10 questions every dad should ask and every young man should be prepared to answer before engagement (way before!)*, both written by her husband and best friend, Dr. Paul A. Friesen.

Other books and study guides
authored or co-authored by Paul or Virginia Friesen
and available from Home Improvement Ministries:

Restoring the Fallen, InterVarsity Press

Letters to My Daughters, Home Improvement Ministries

So You Want to Marry My Daughter?, Home Improvement Ministries

Recapturing Eden, Home Improvement Ministries

Engagement Matters, Home Improvement Ministries

In Our Image, Home Improvement Ministries

~

For more information about Home Improvement Ministries, or to book Paul
and Virginia Friesen for a speaking engagement, or to order any of our products,
please write, e-mail, fax, or call us:

Call: 781-275-6473
Fax: 781-275-6469
E-mail: info@himweb.org
Write: Home Improvement Ministries
          209 Burlington Road, Suite 105
          Bedford, MA 01730 USA
Online: www.HIMweb.org/books (for the online bookstore)
          www.HIMweb.org/speak (to book the Friesens for speaking)